LETTER COLORING
ACTIVITY BOOK

Author/Designer MsBe

Greetings

Make copies of the designed pages in this book. Select letters that represent your initials, spell out your name or a special message. Next enjoy coloring the letters. This was prepared for your personal use.

Consider framing each letter for a dramatic effect. There are attractive $1 frames you can purchase. A wonderful gift idea. See samples below:

FRAME YOUR WORK!!!

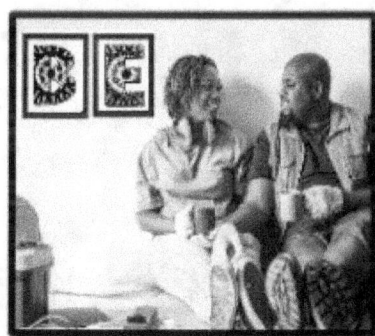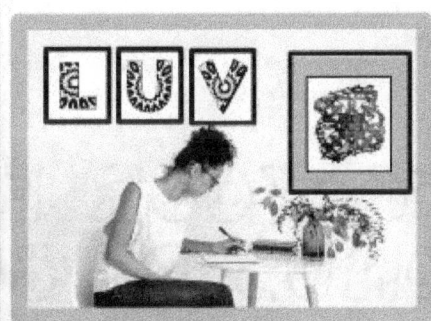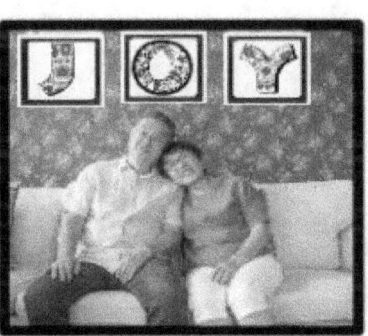

STRING THEM UP!!!

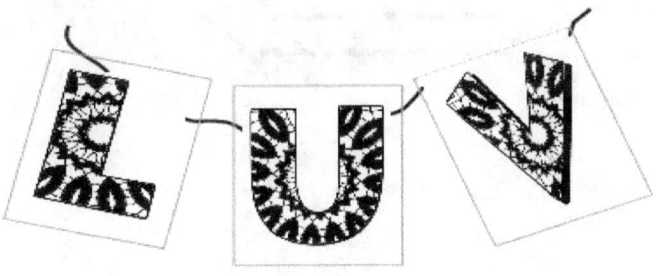

Have Great Days!

MsBe

SPECIAL NOTE:
Place extra paper behind the page as you color, to ensures no bleeding, when using markers.

ENJOY YOUR FIRST BONUS PAGE!

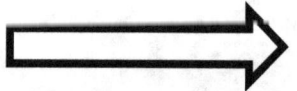

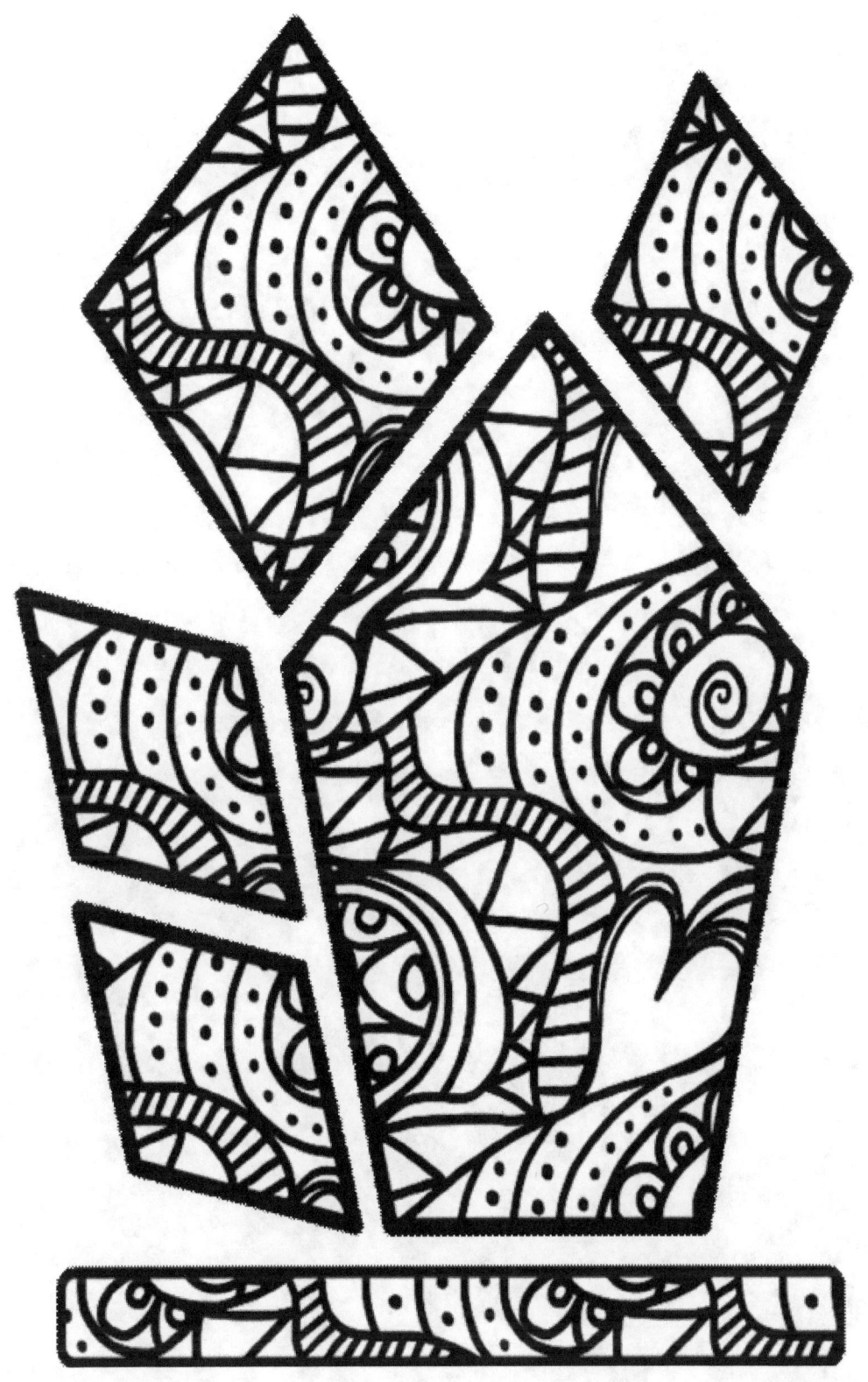

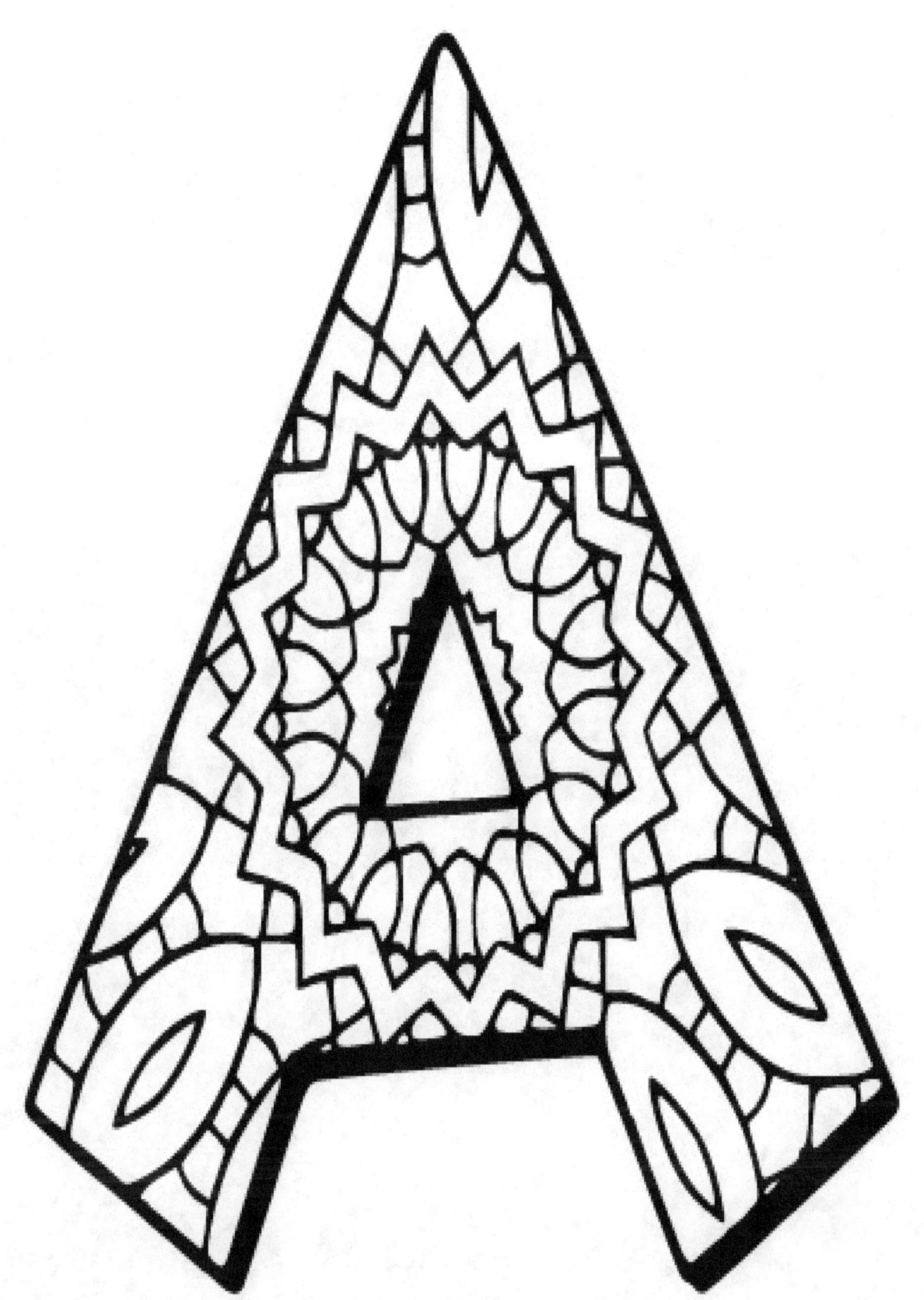

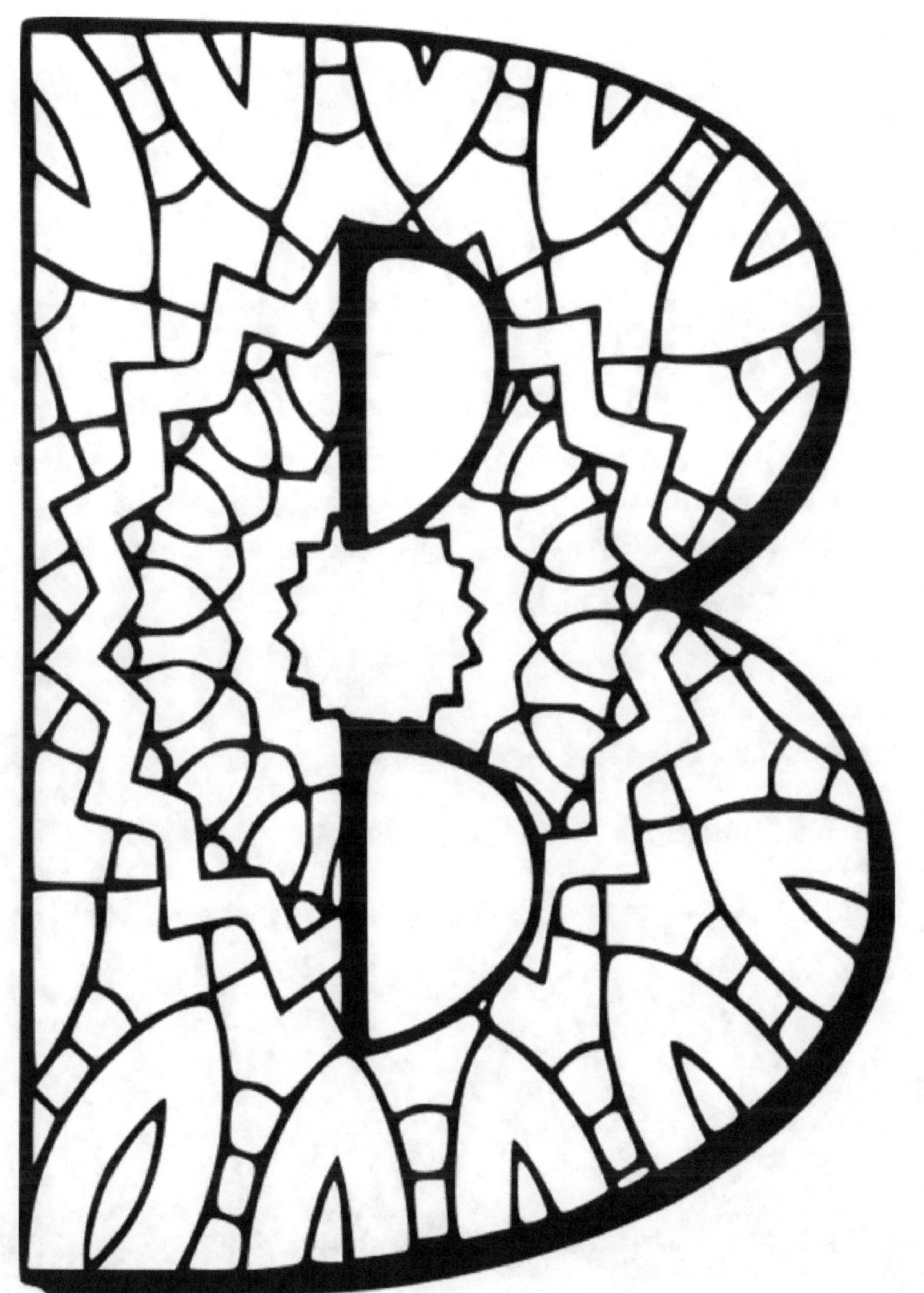

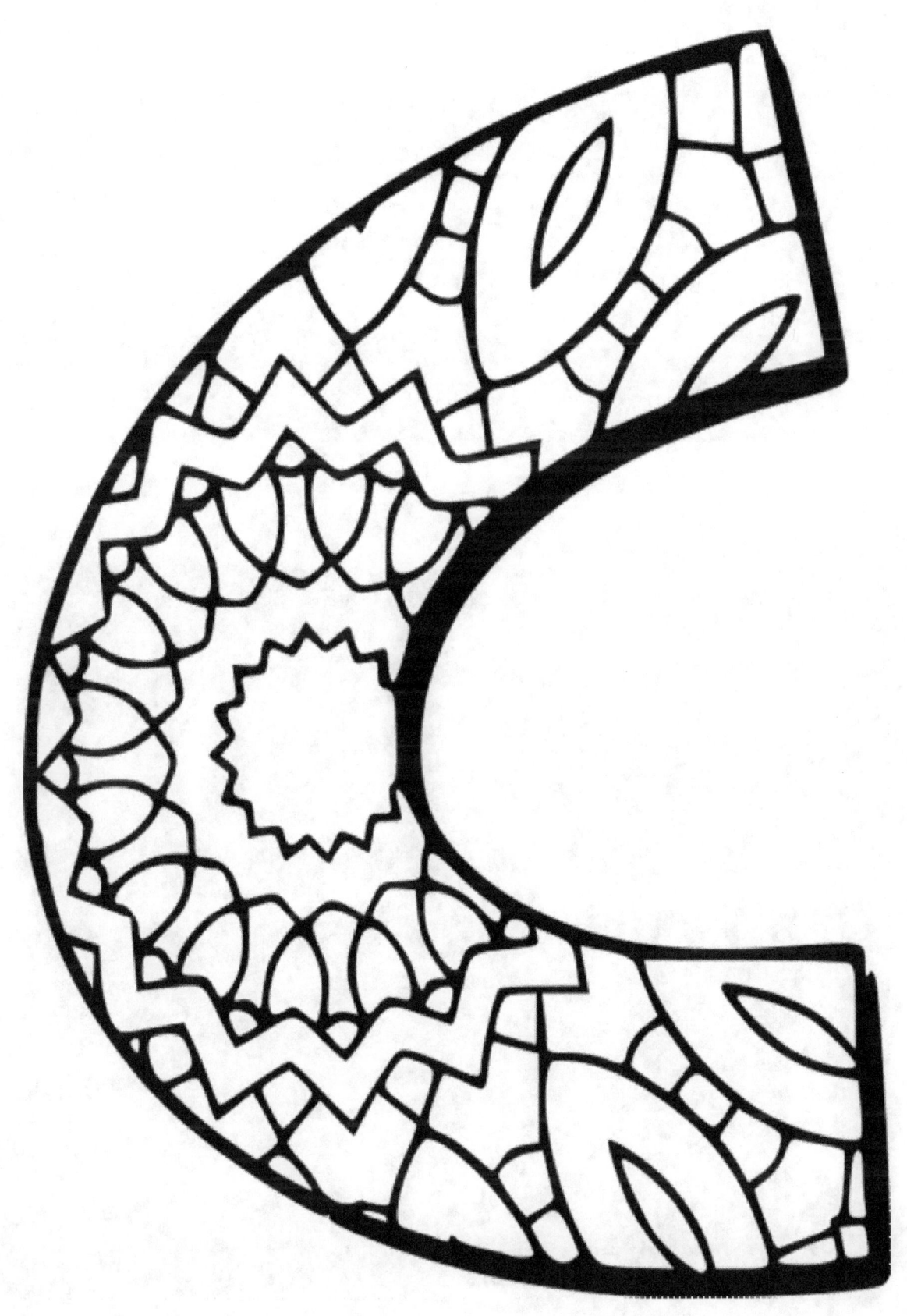

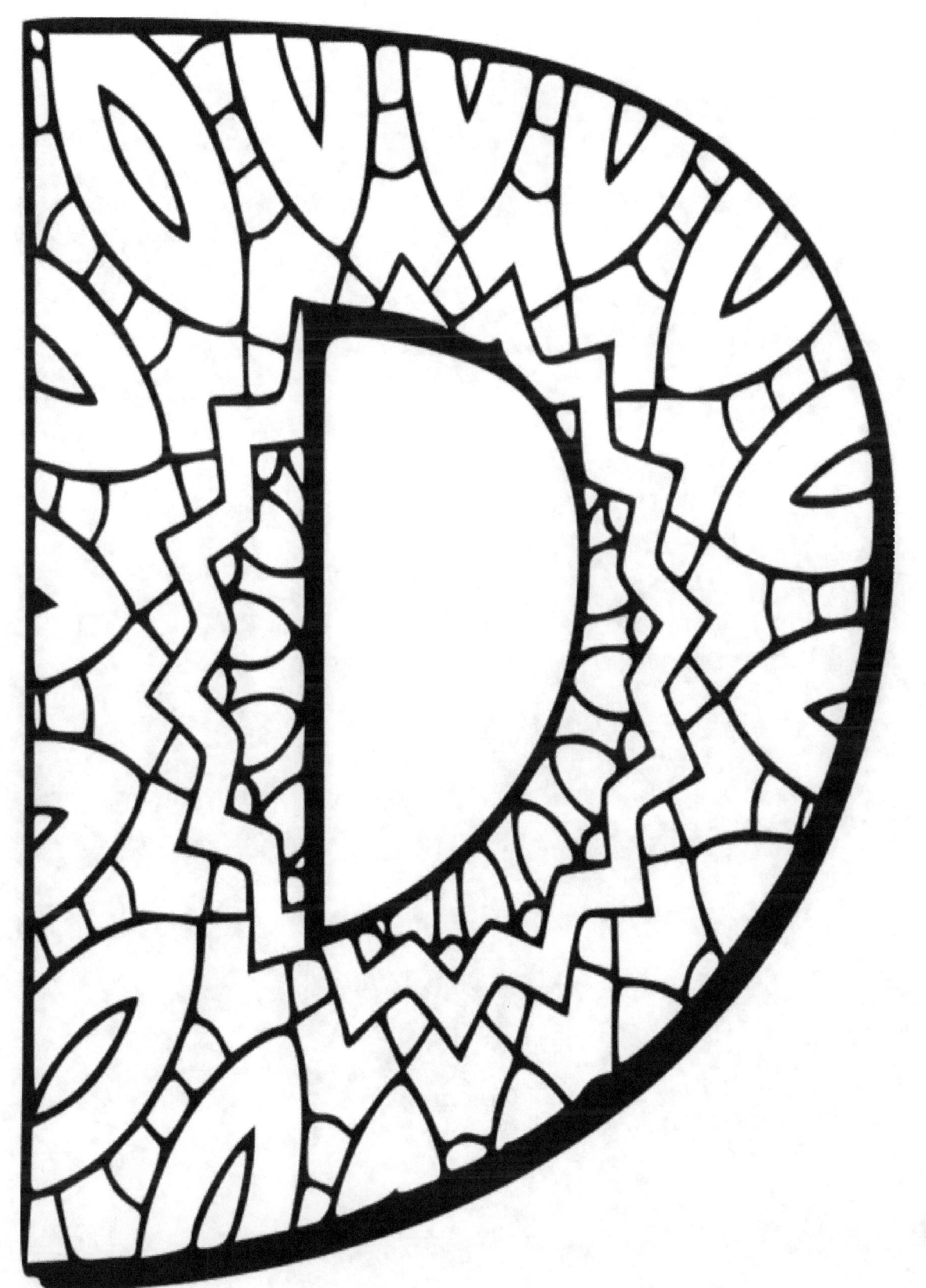

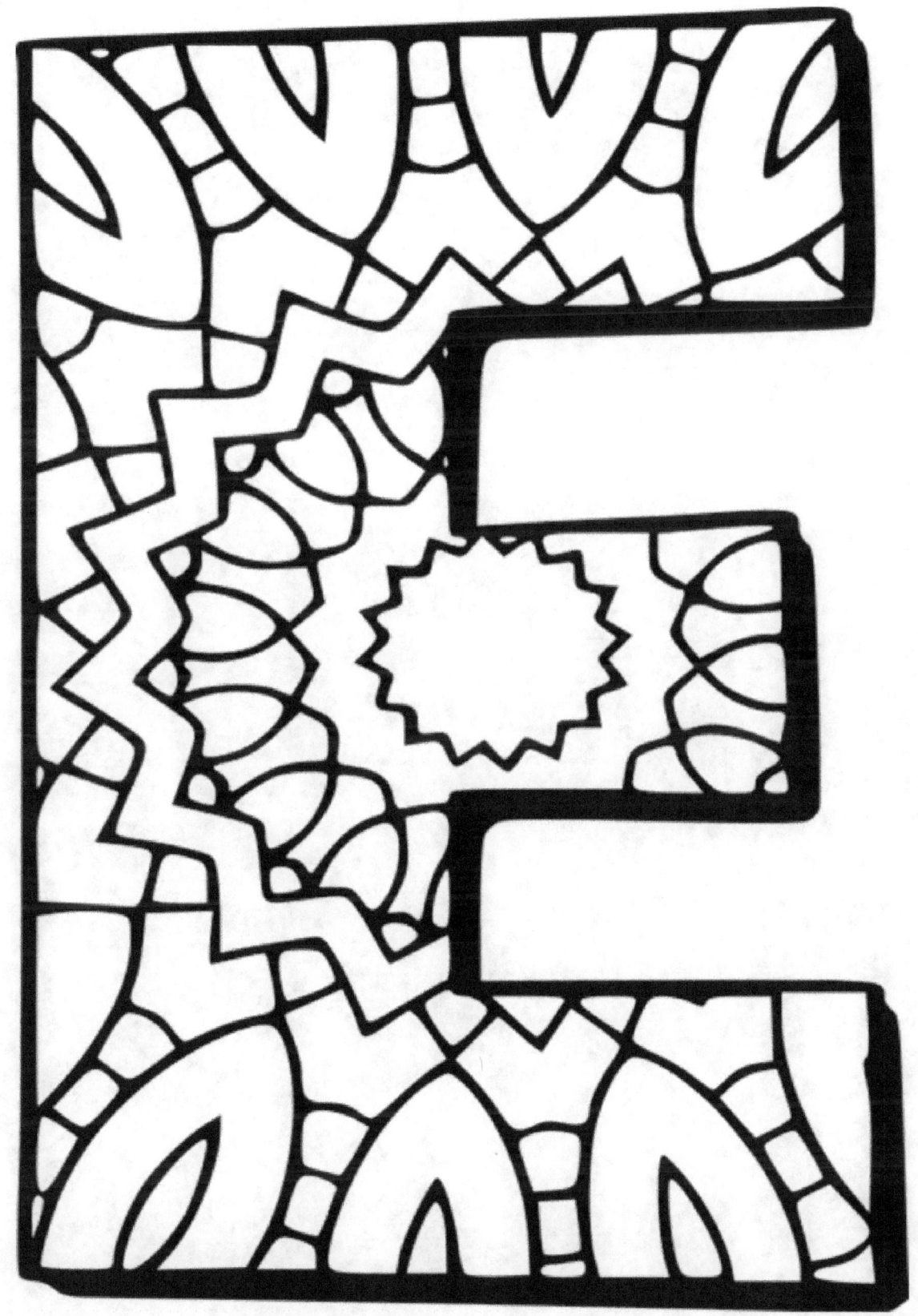

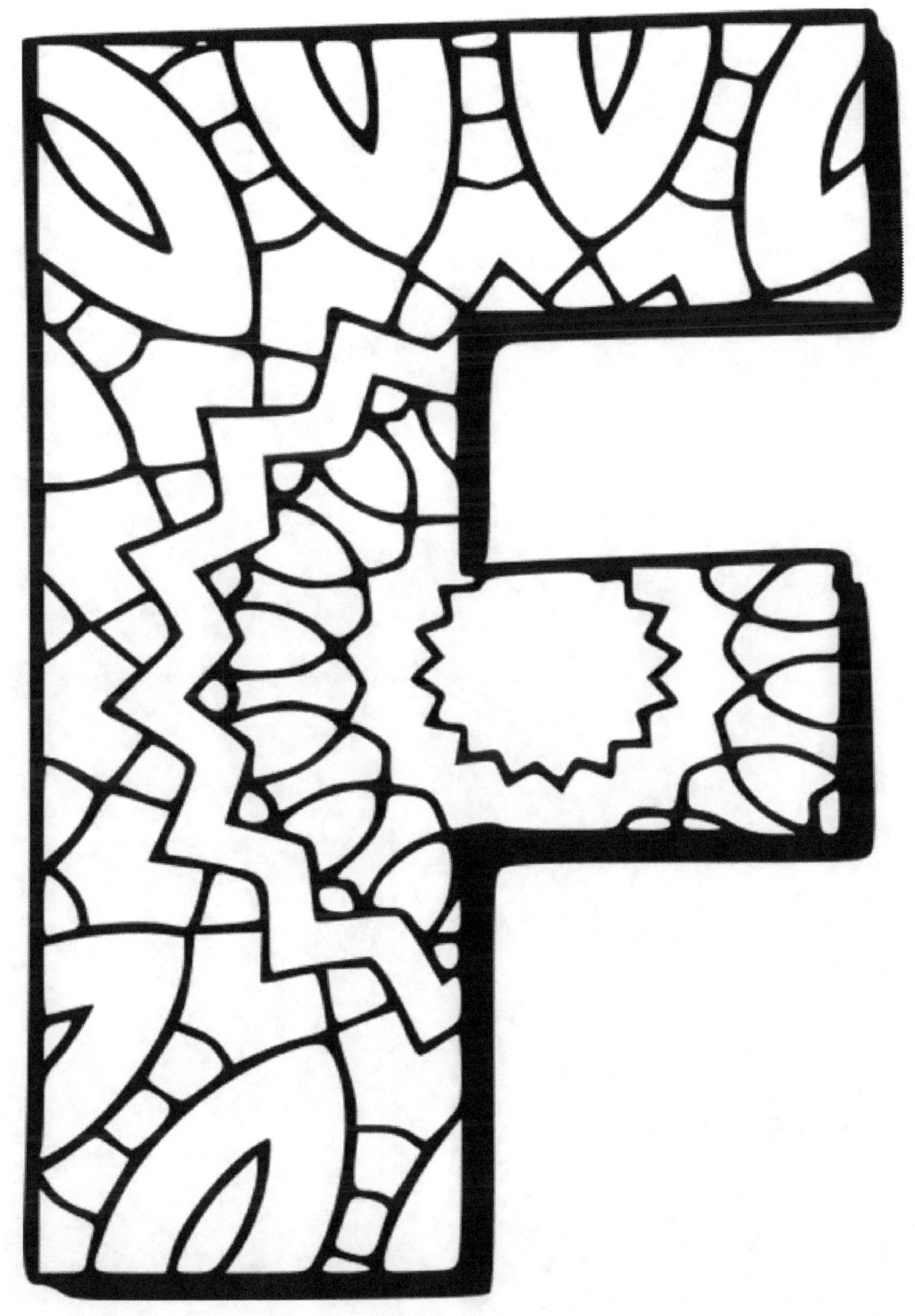

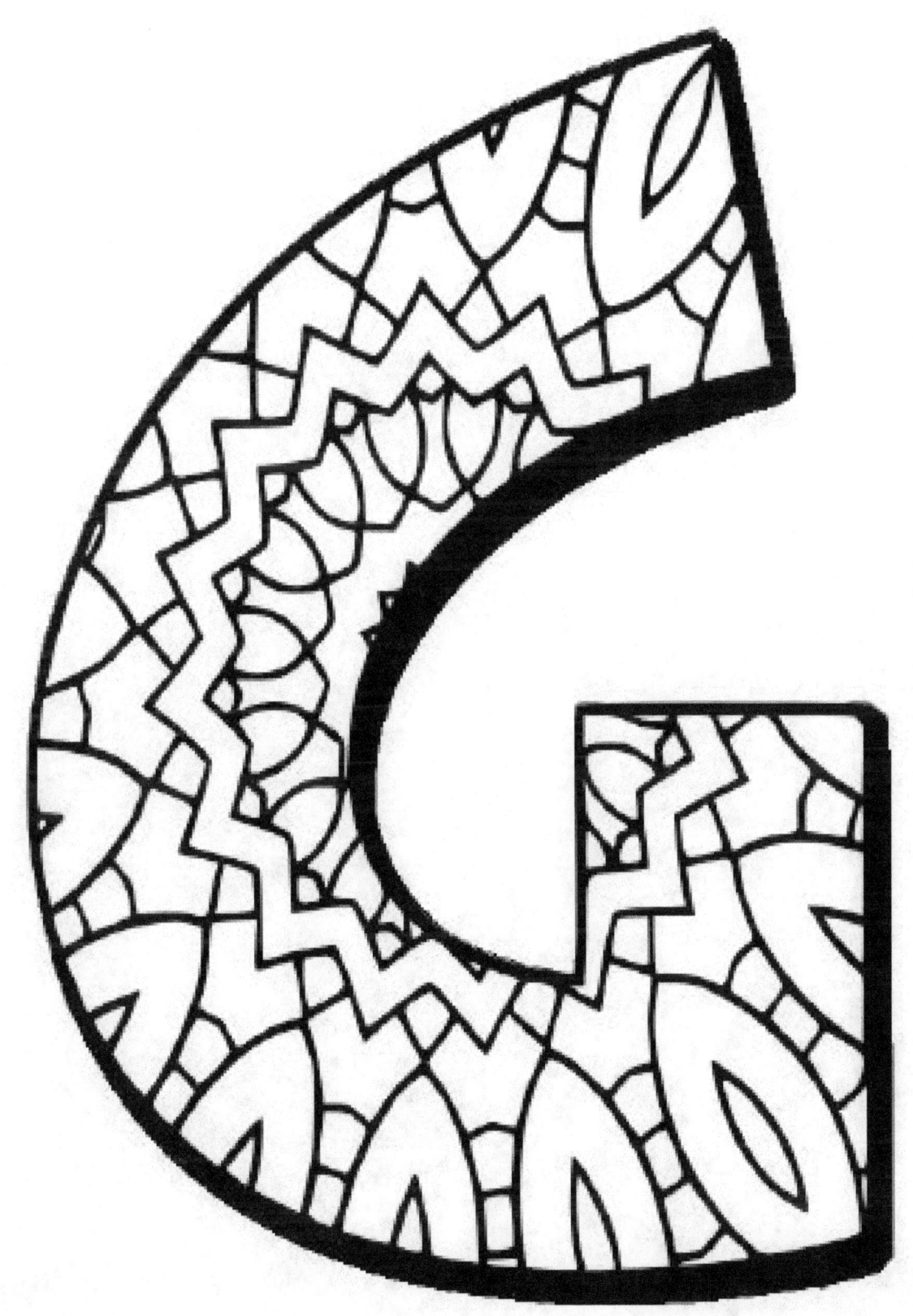

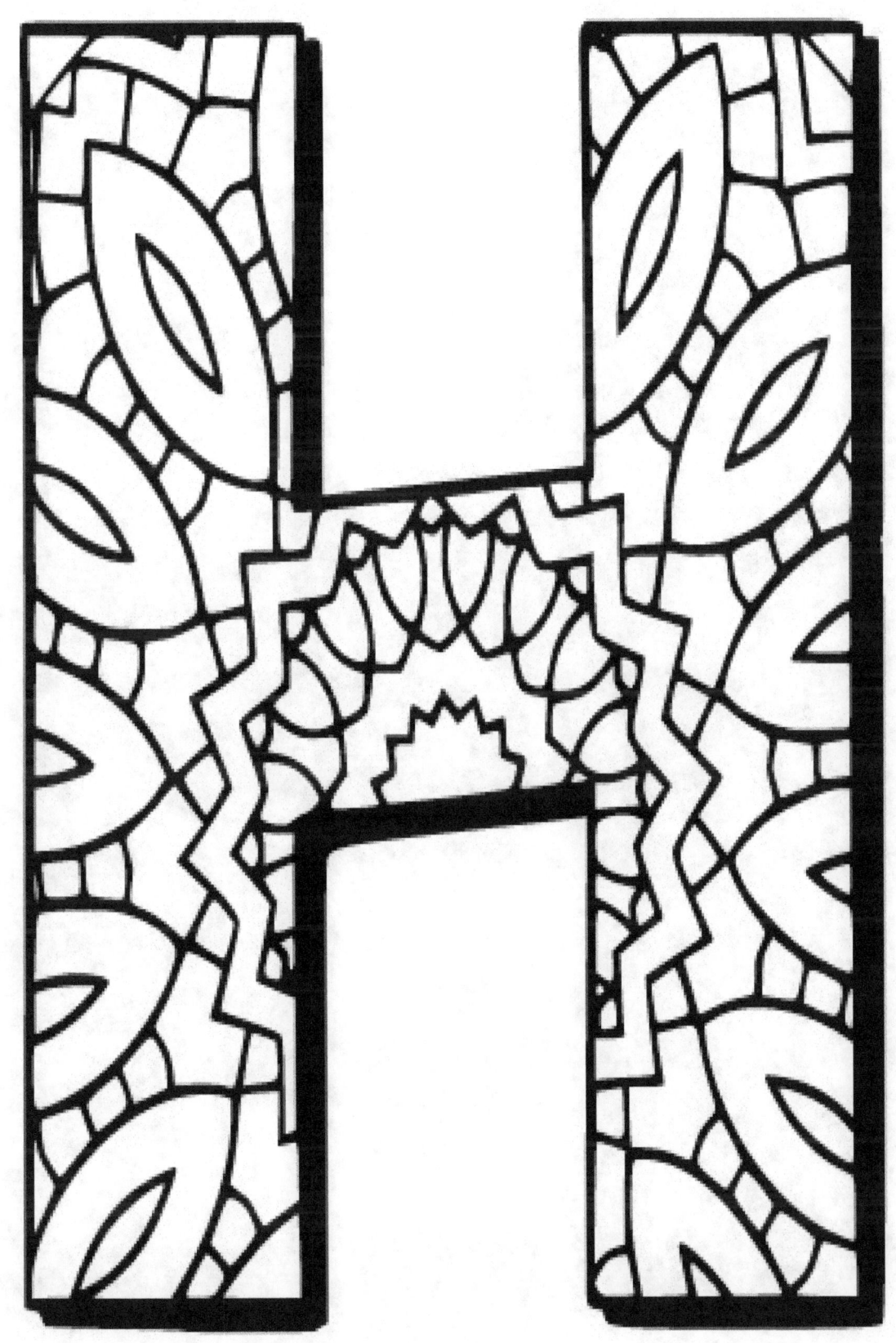

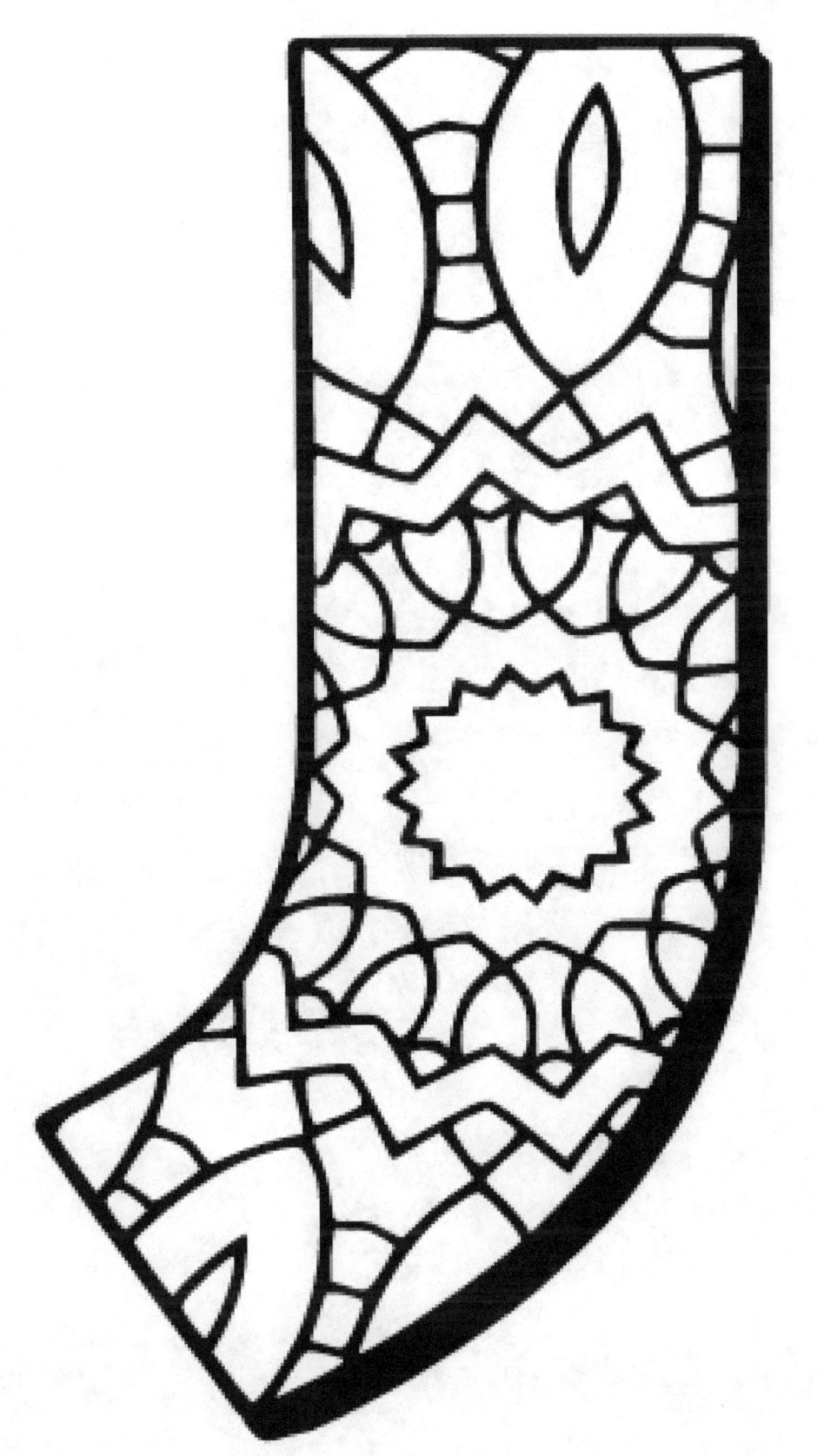

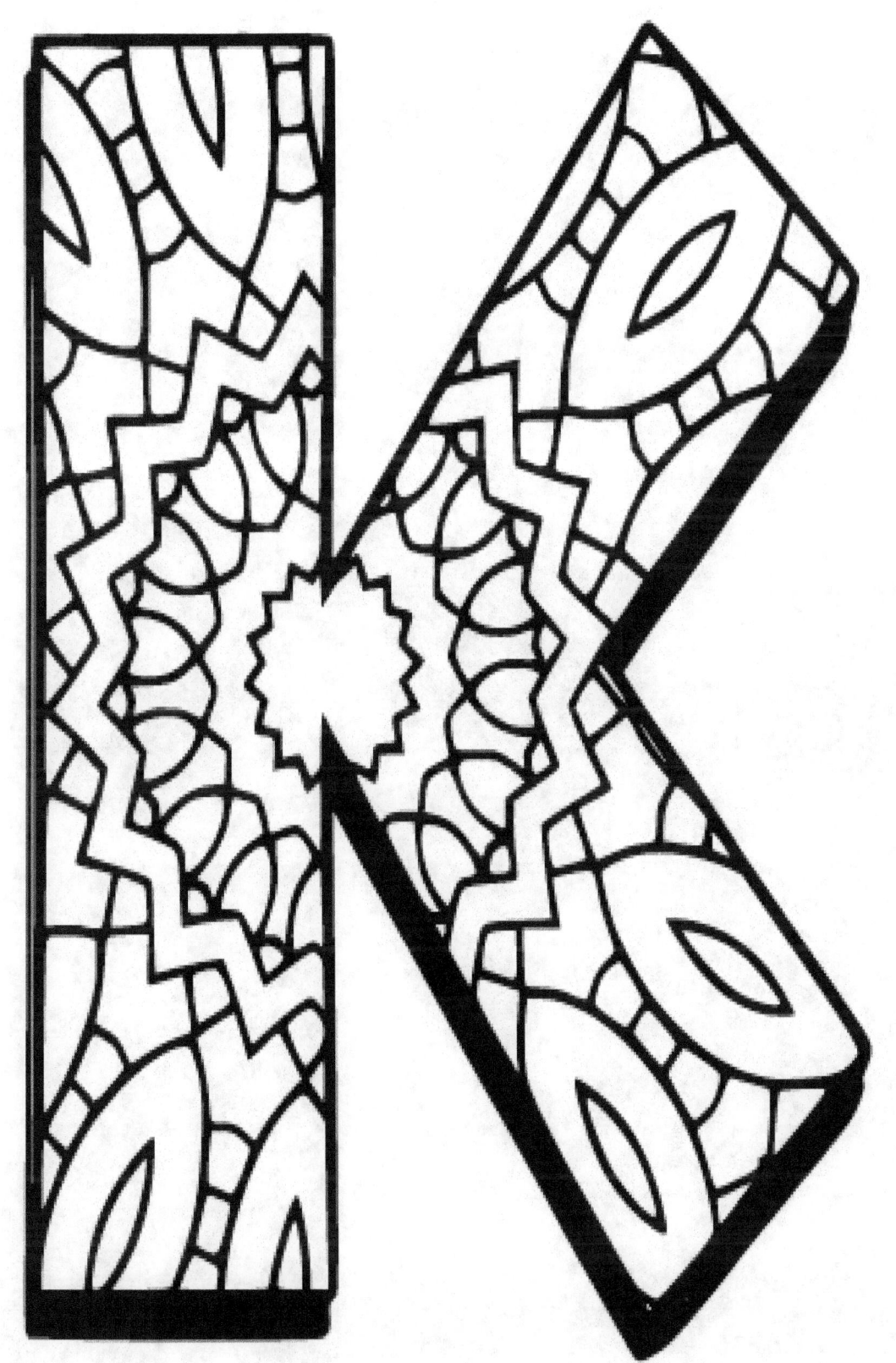

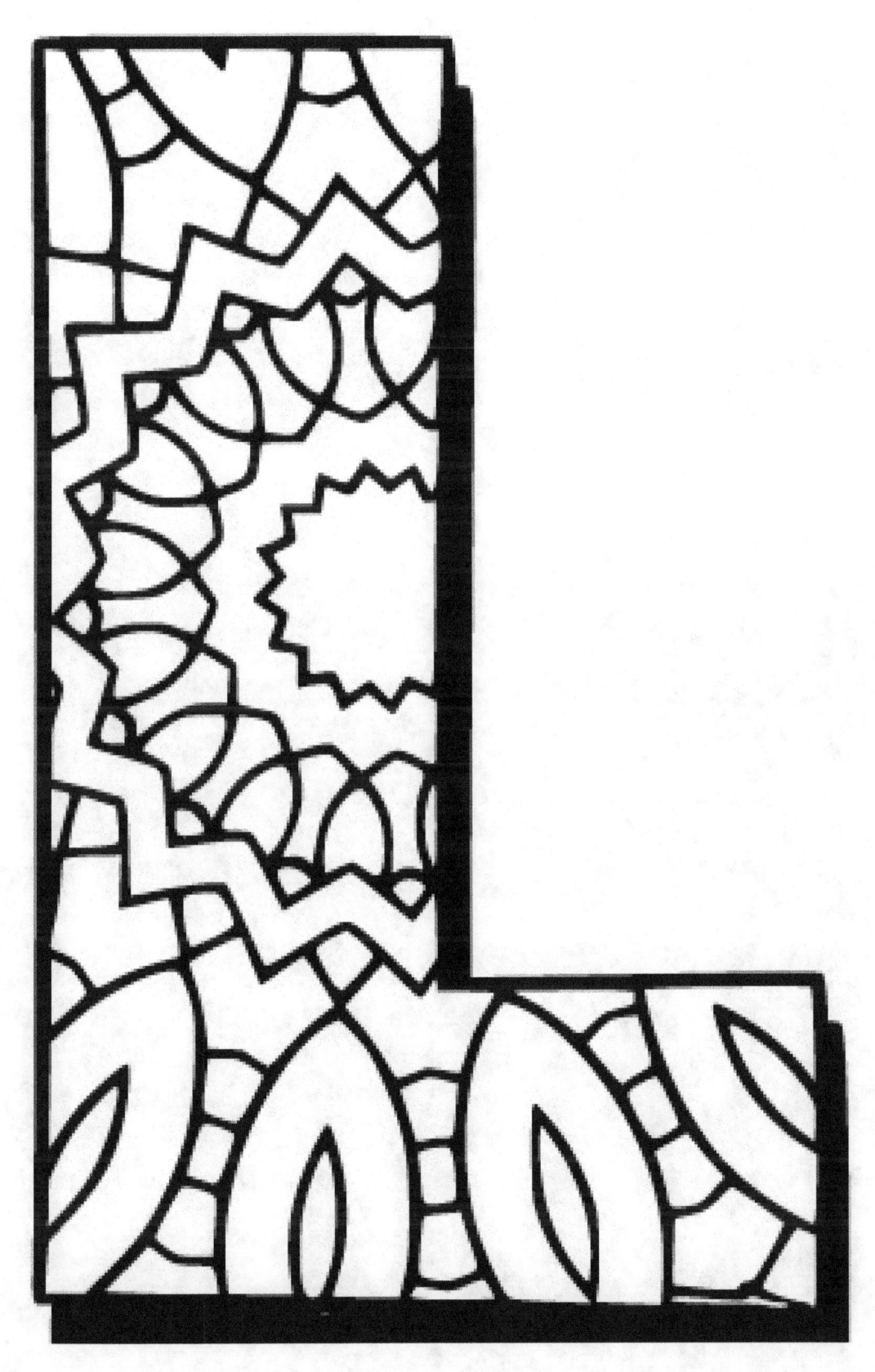

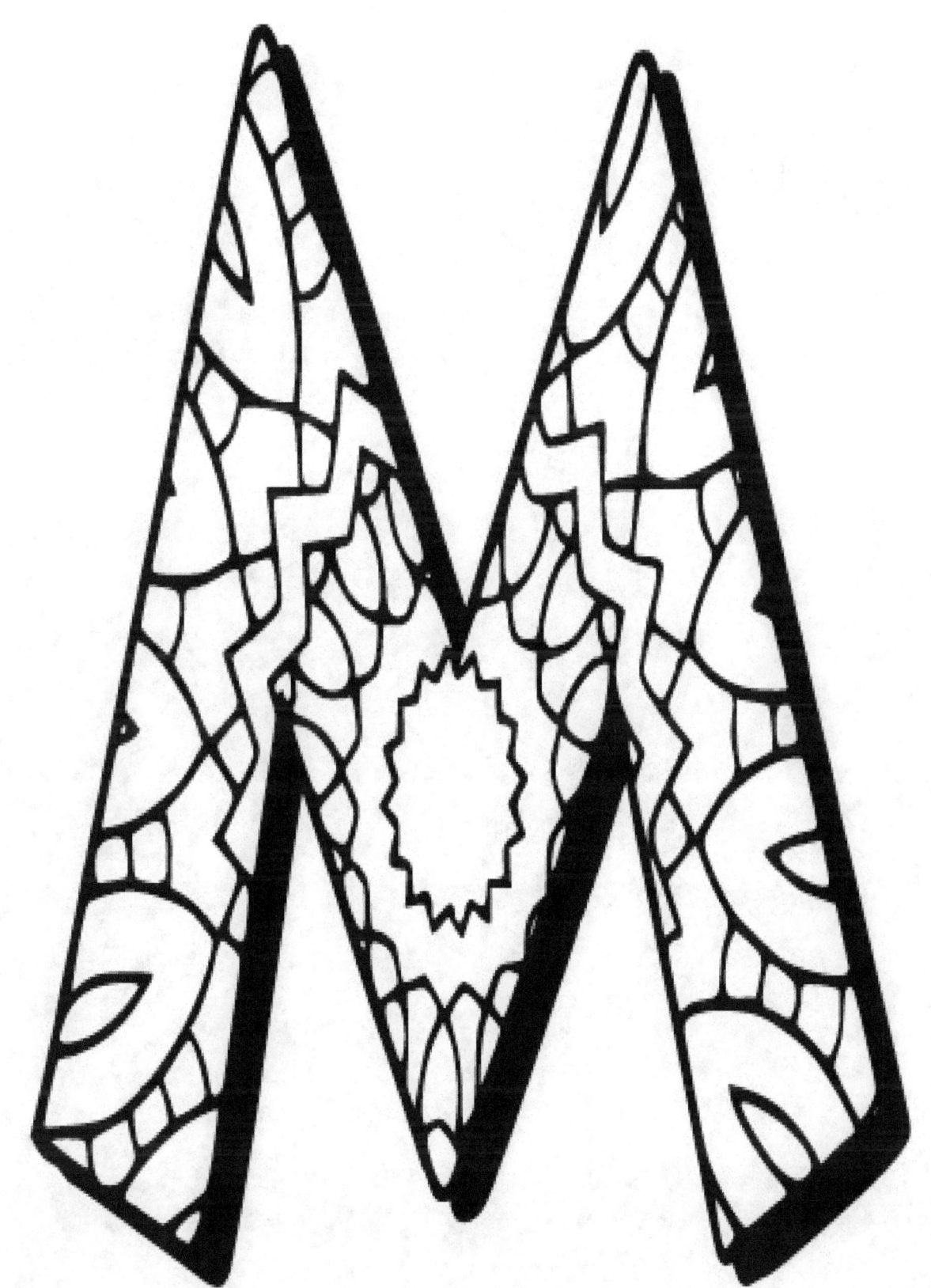

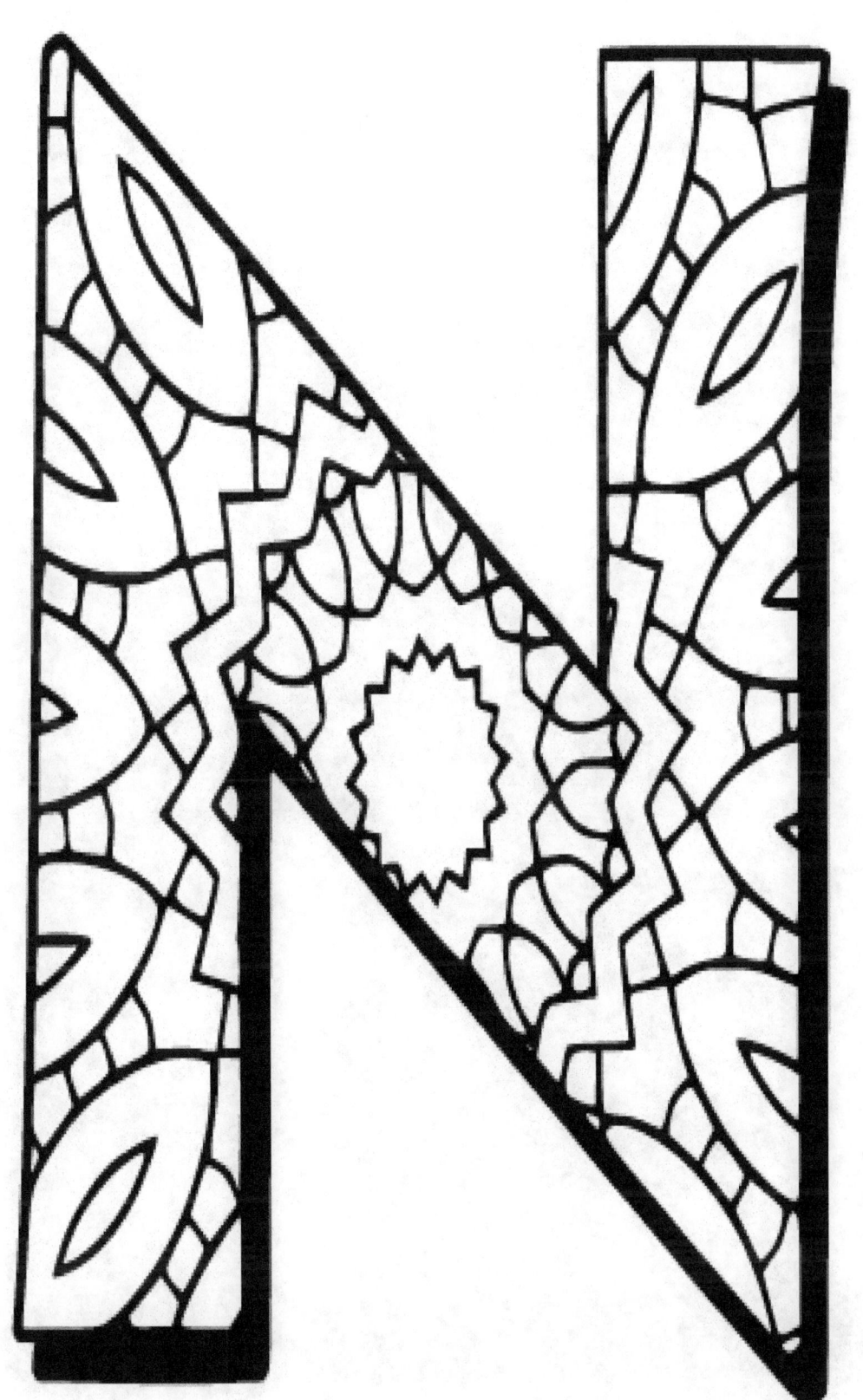

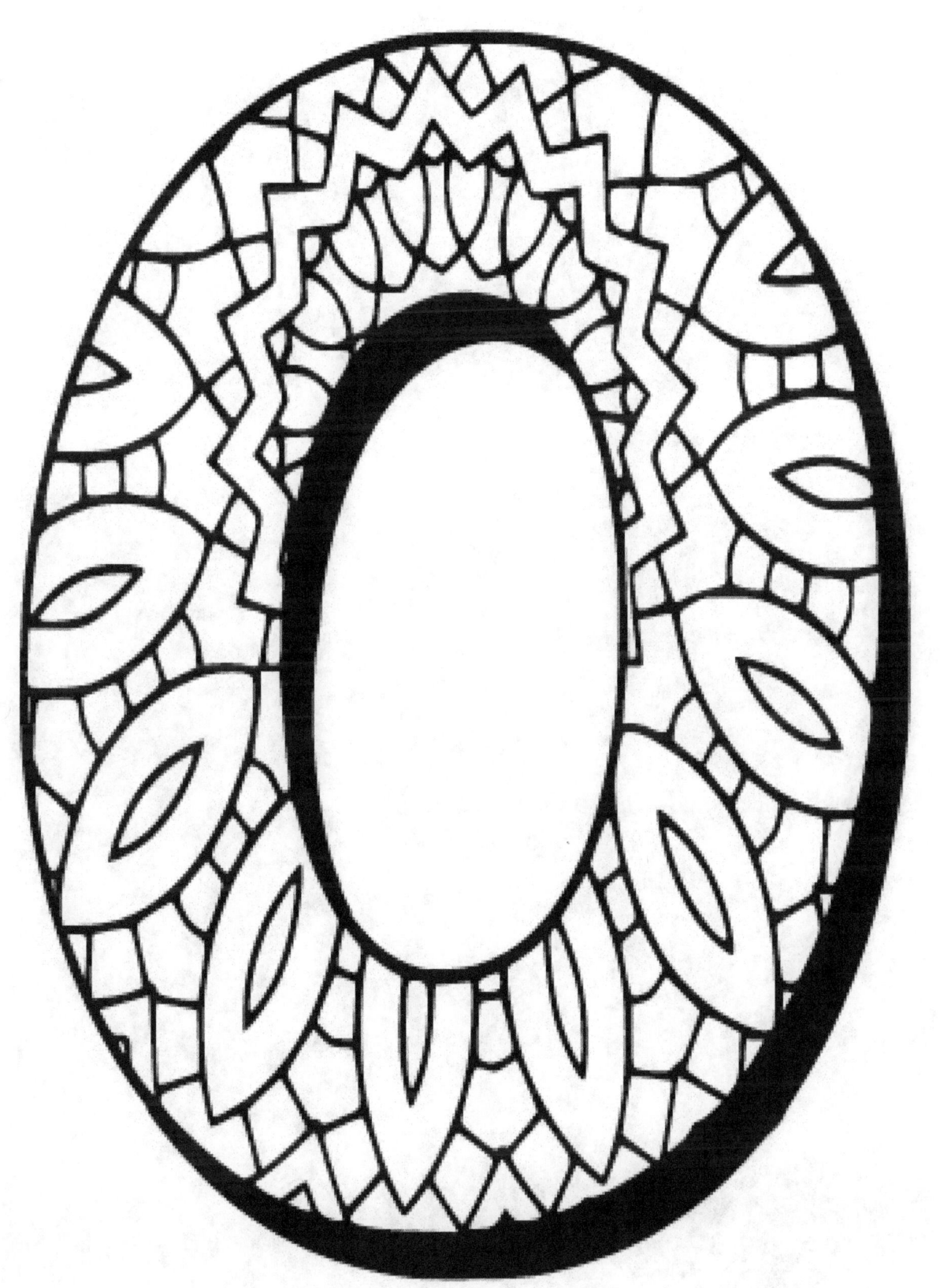

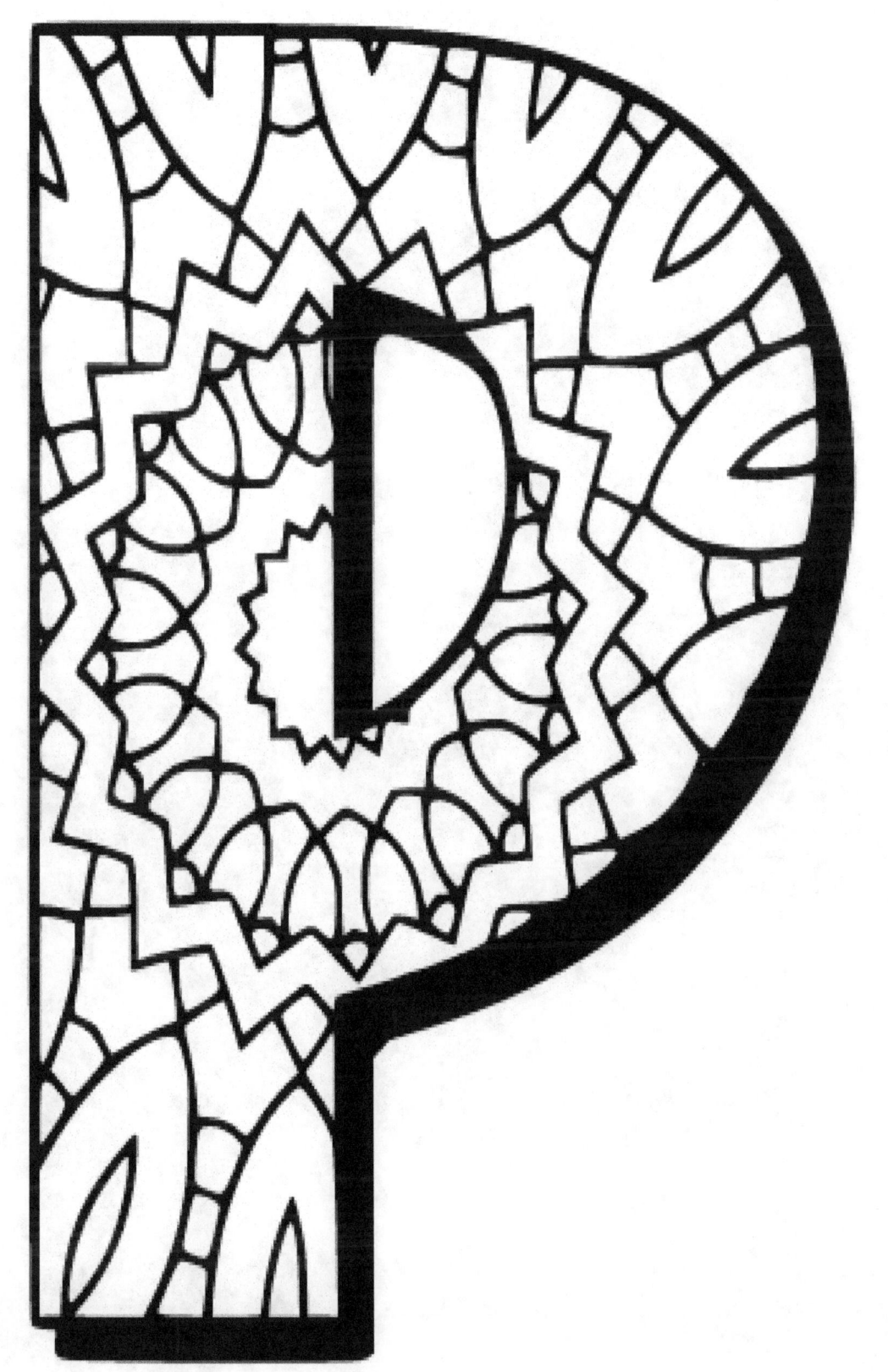

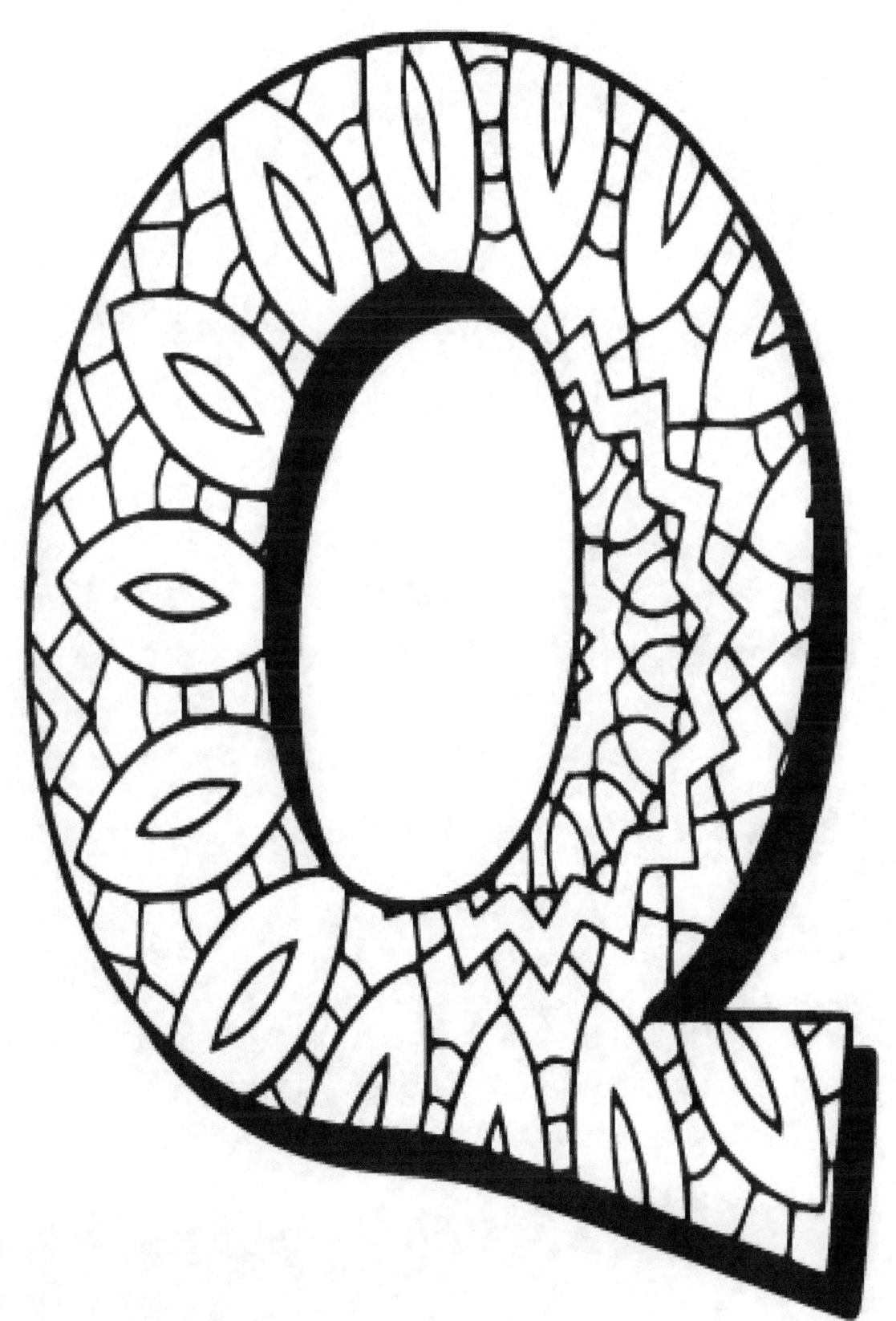

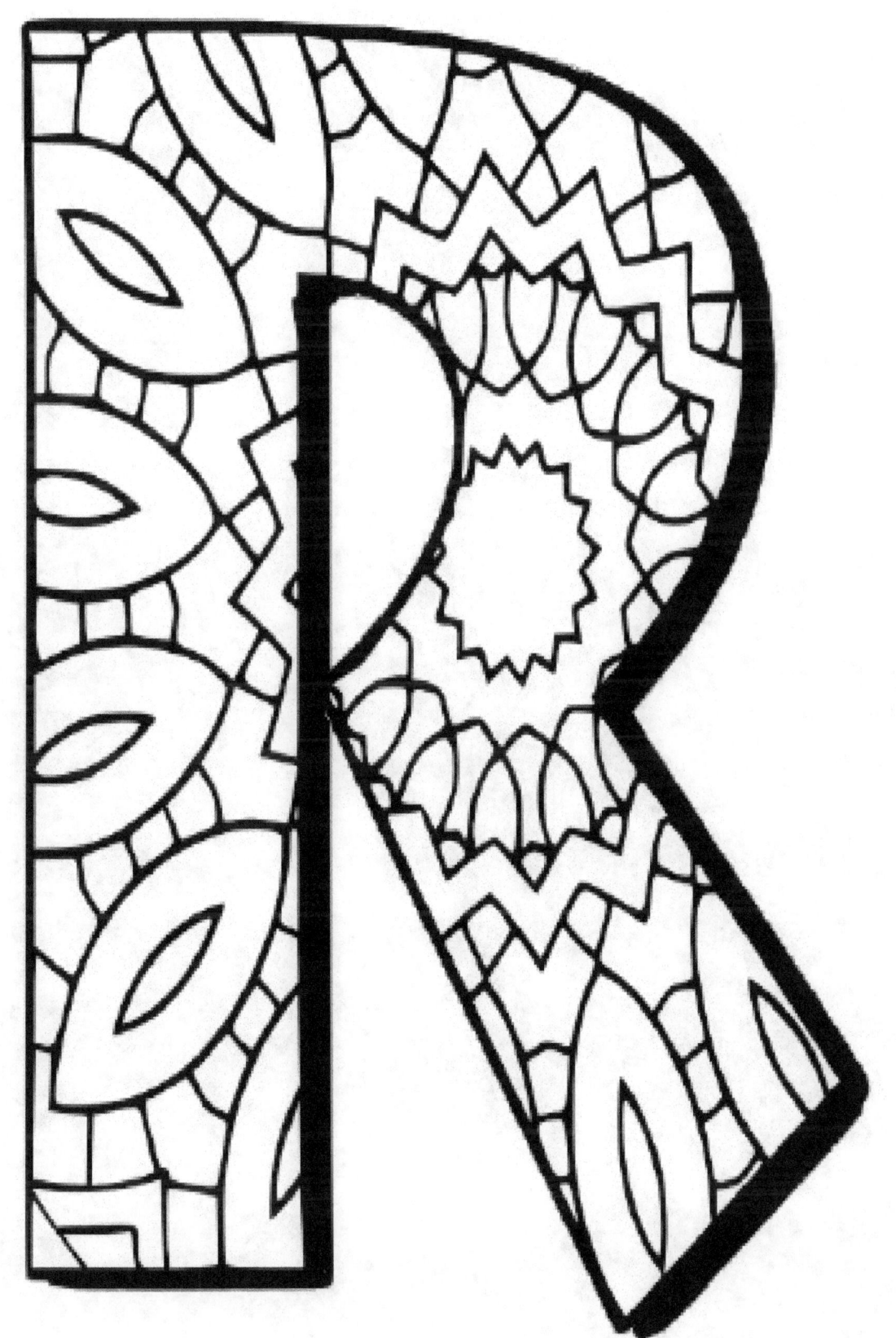

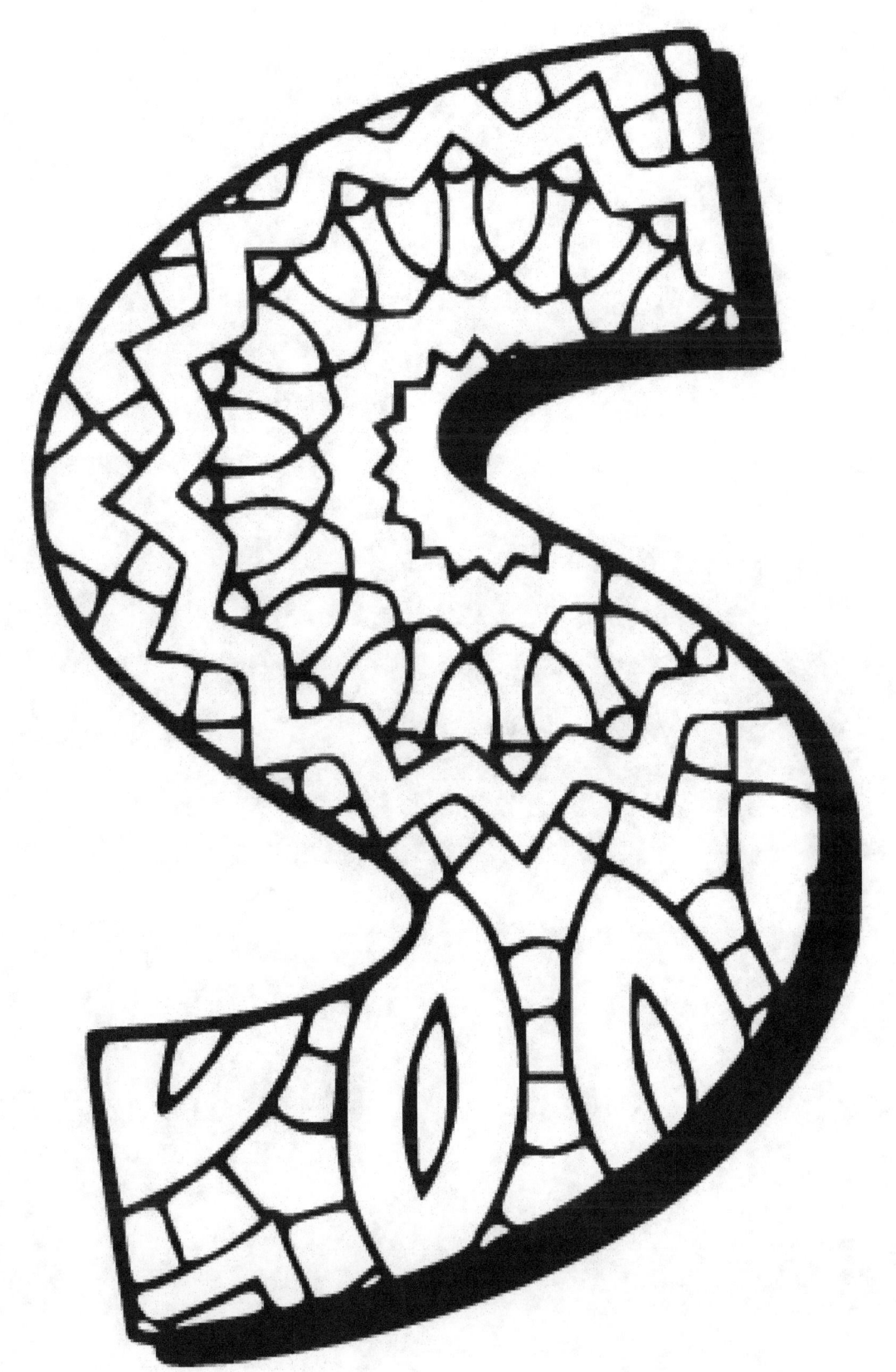

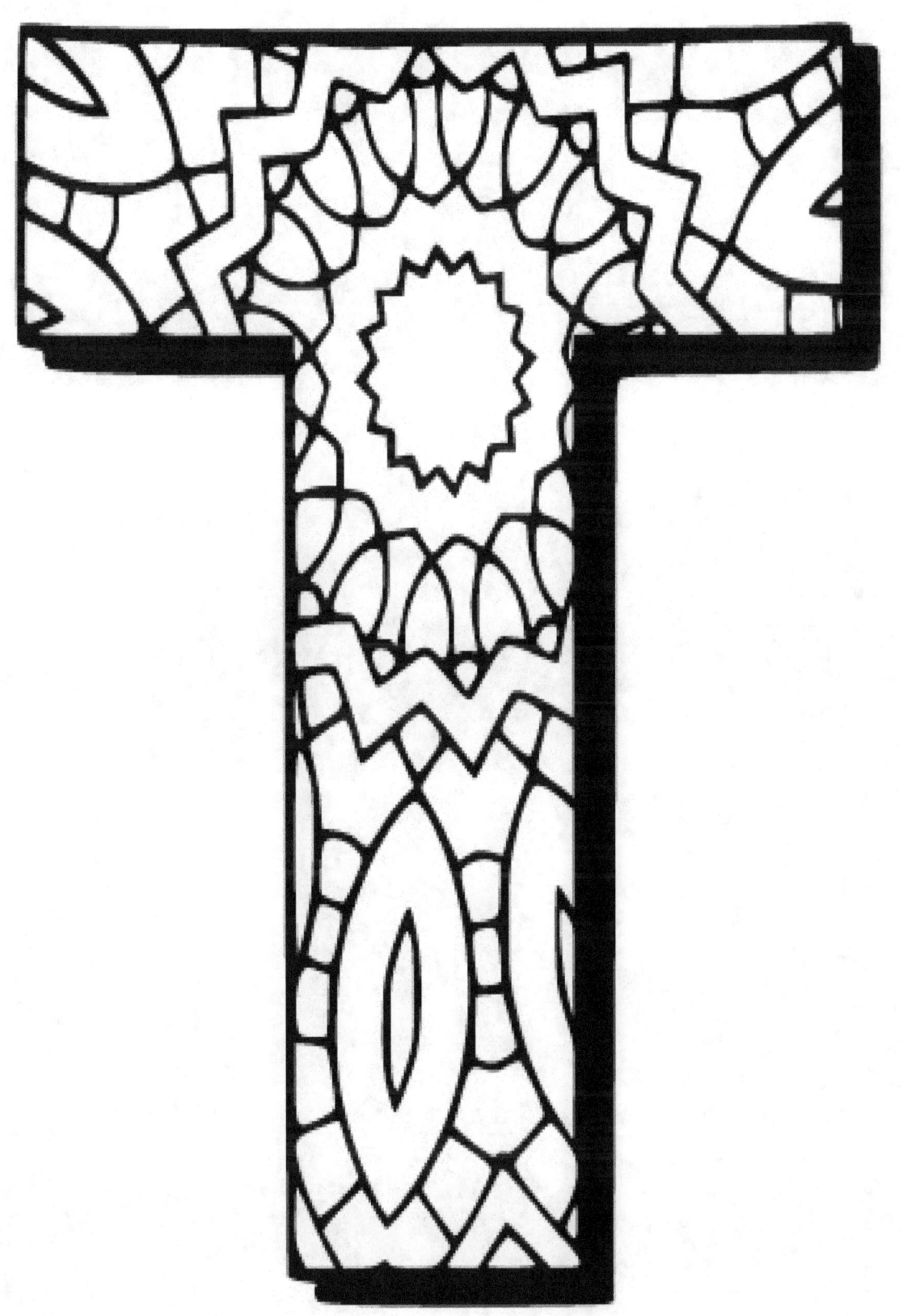

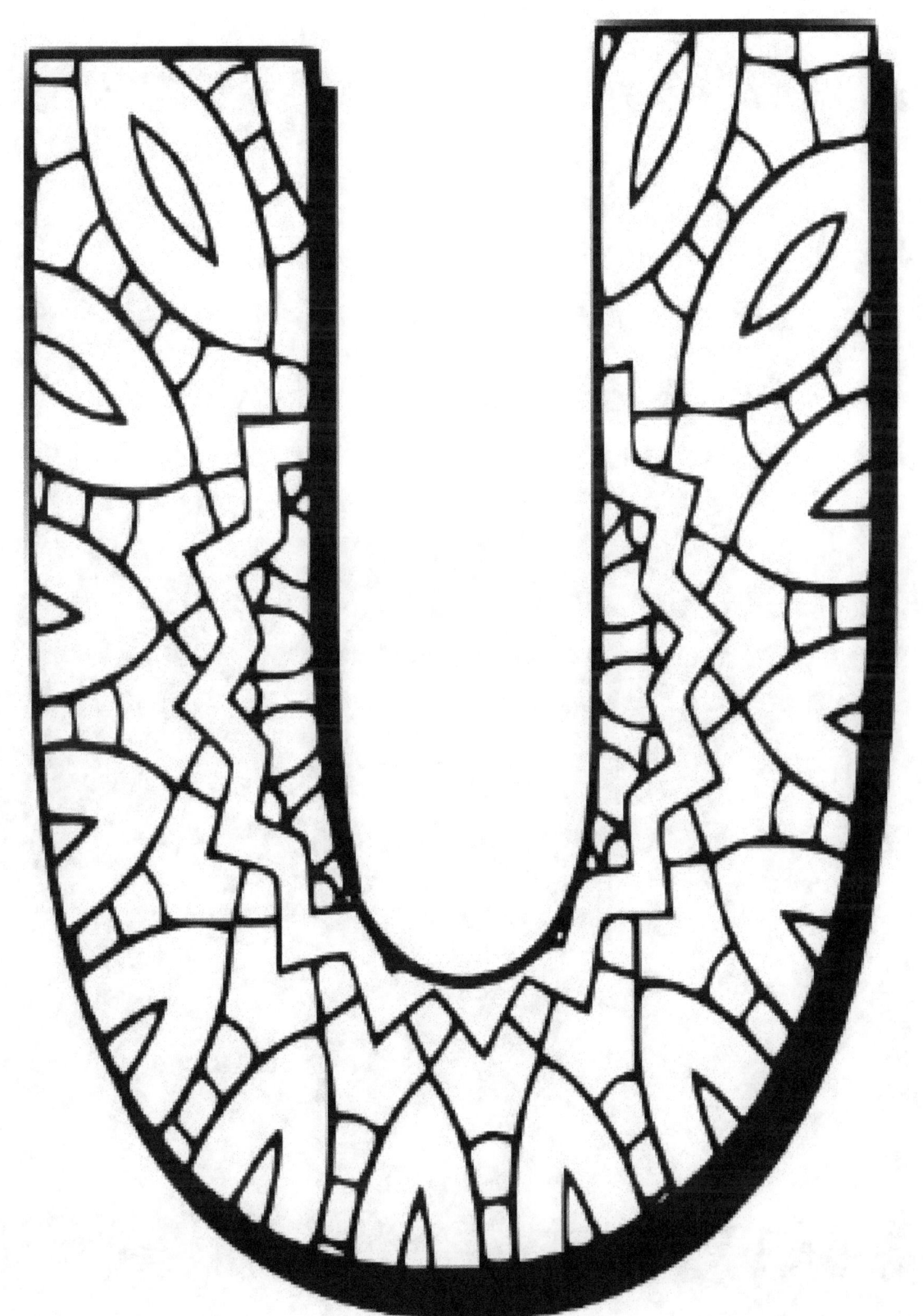

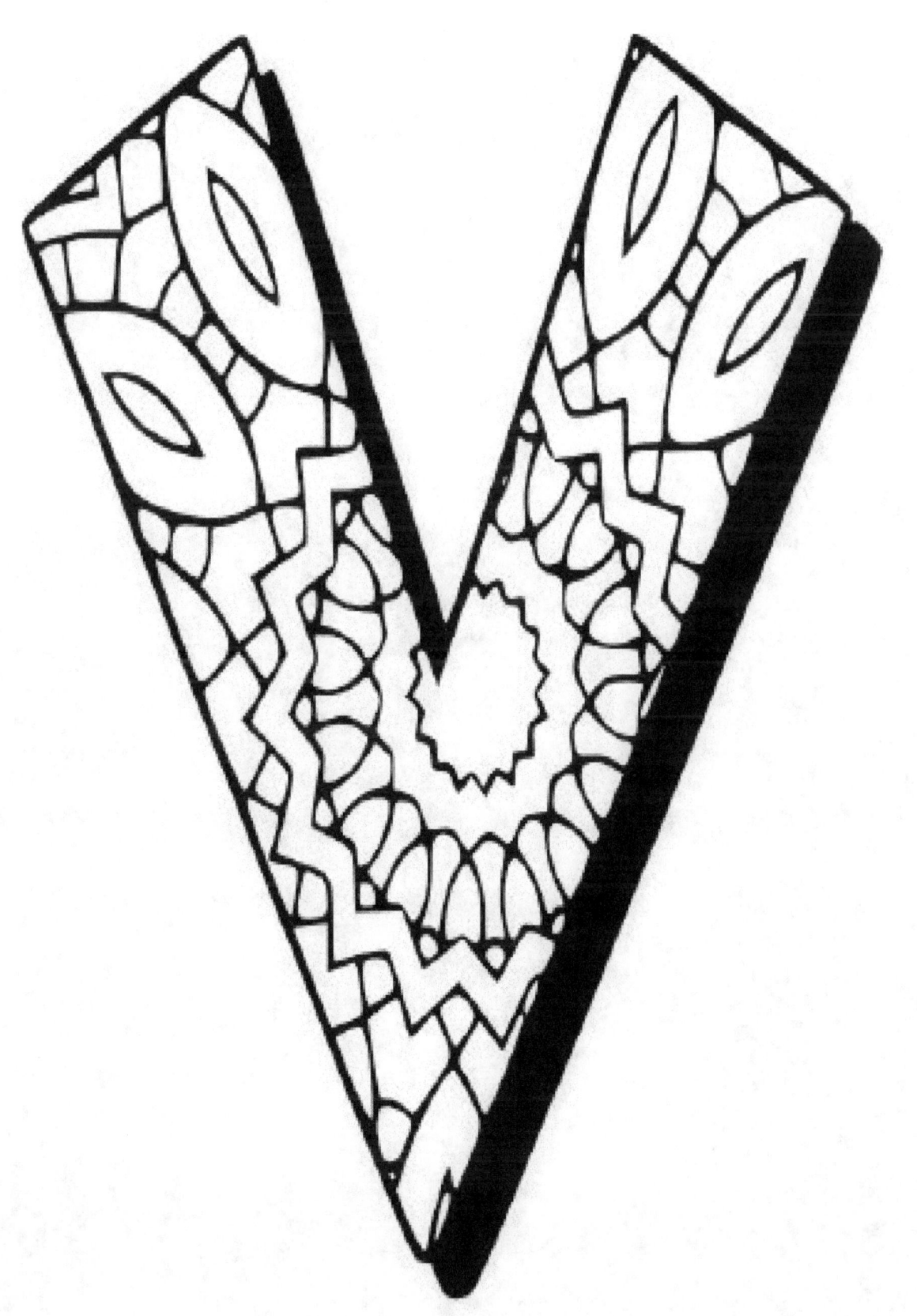

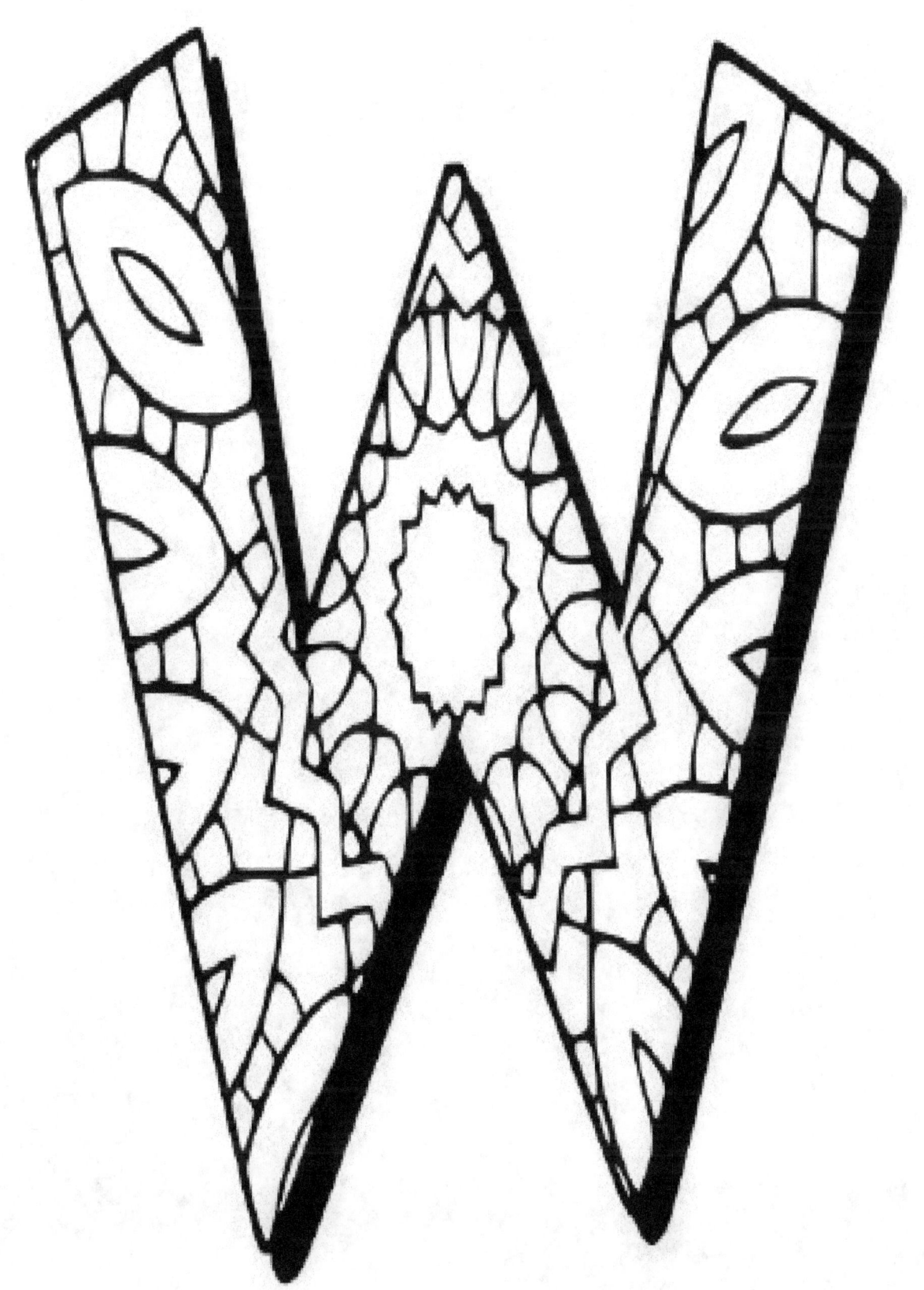

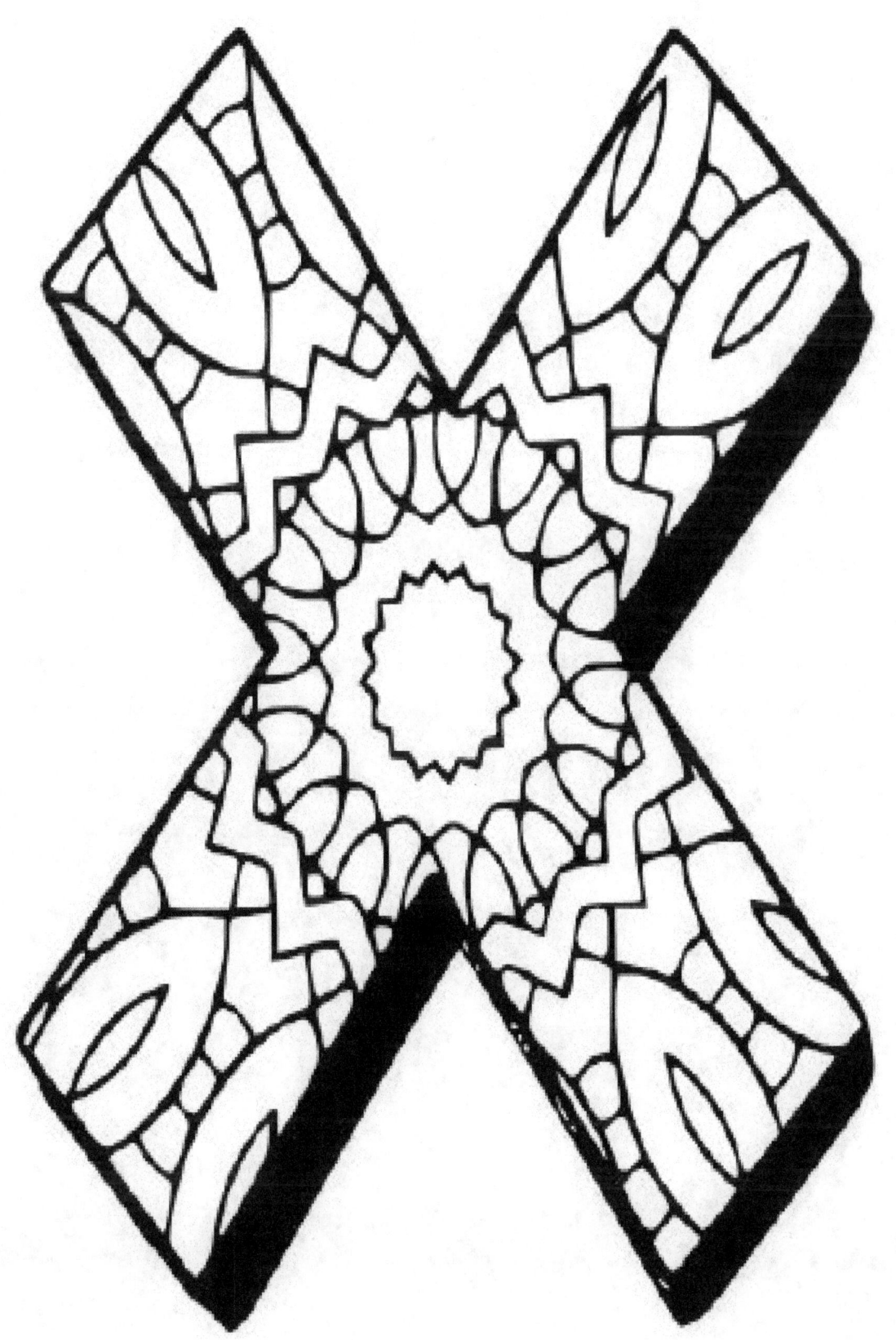

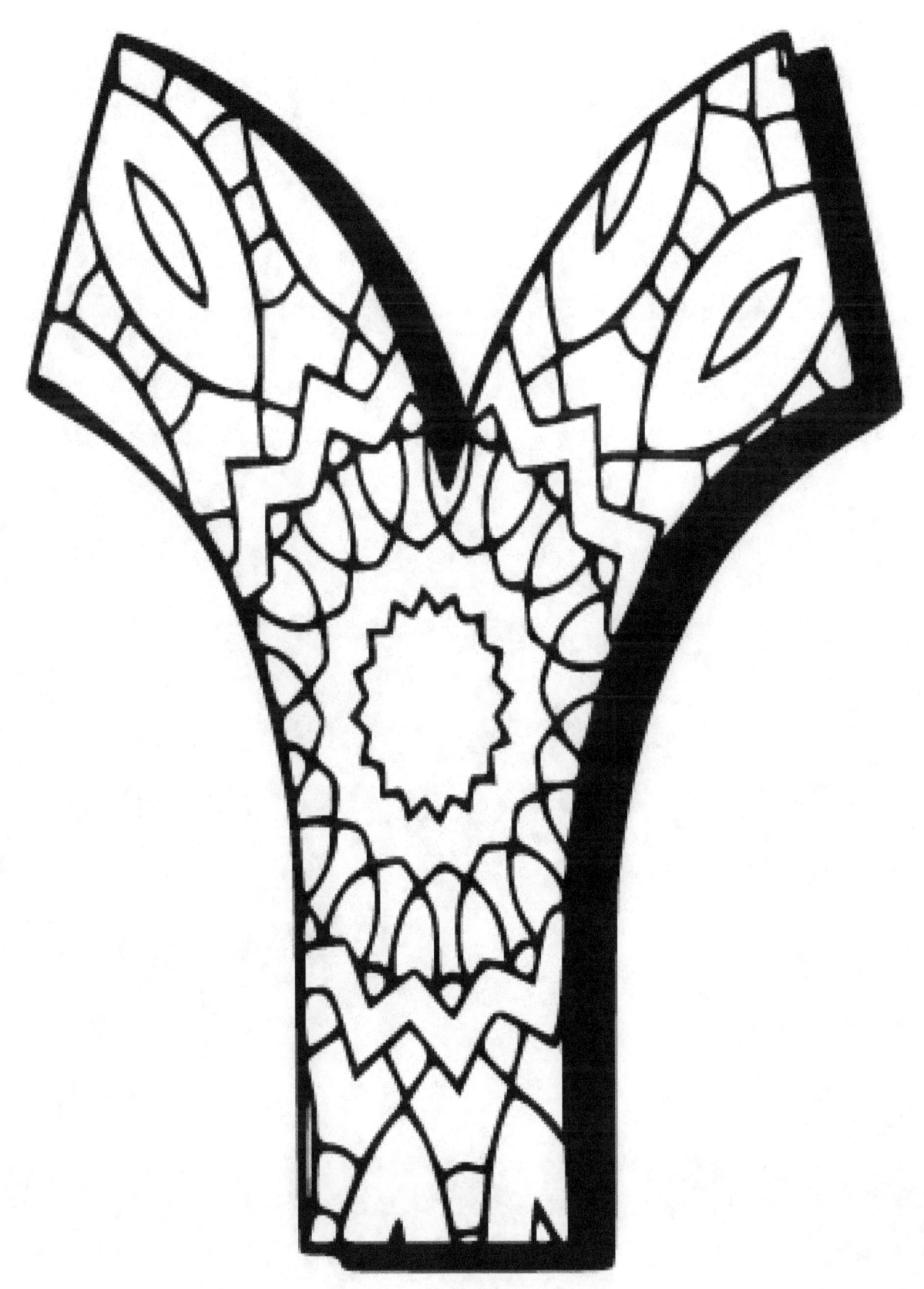

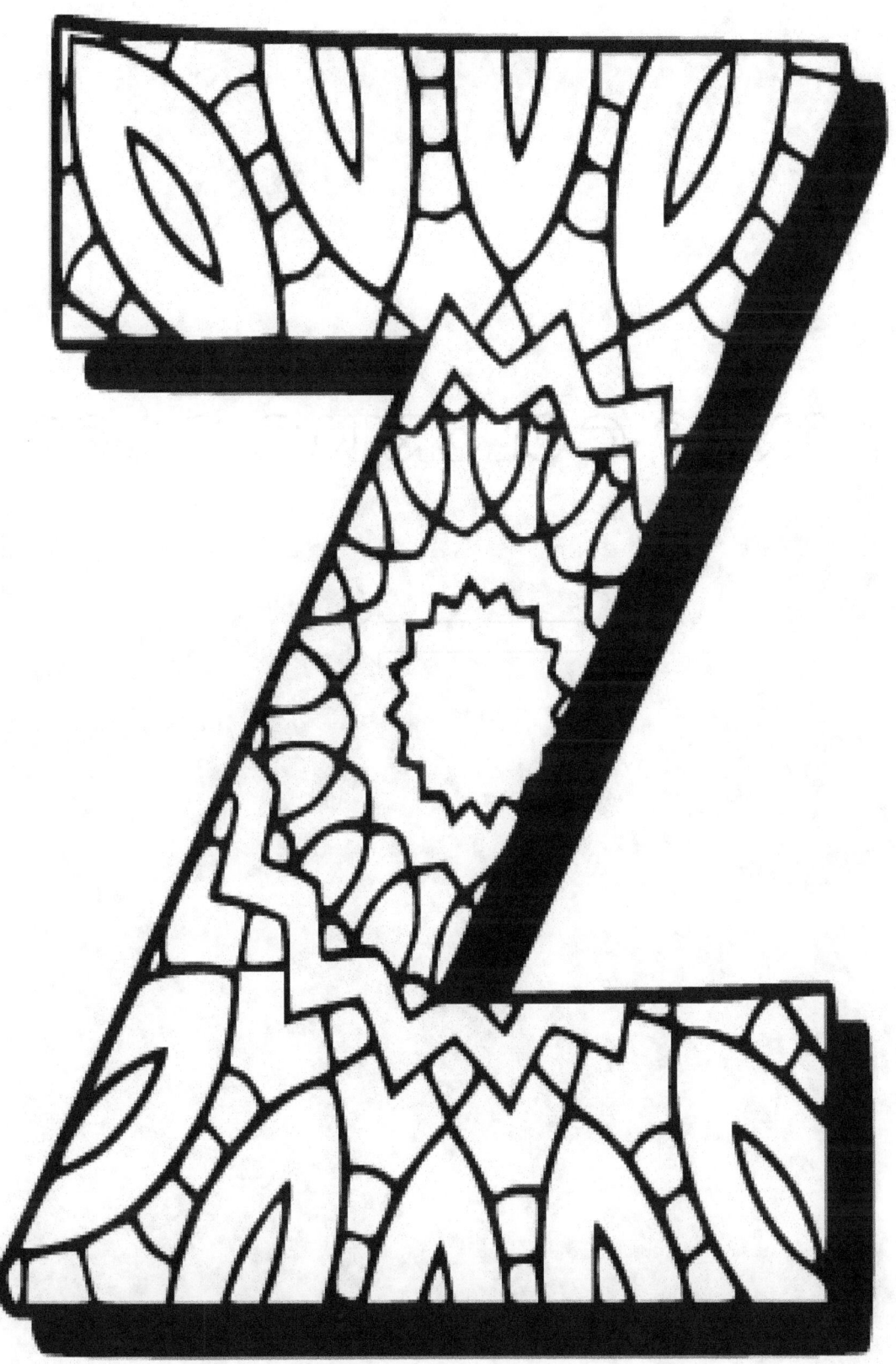

BONUS COLORING PAGES!

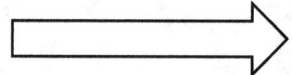

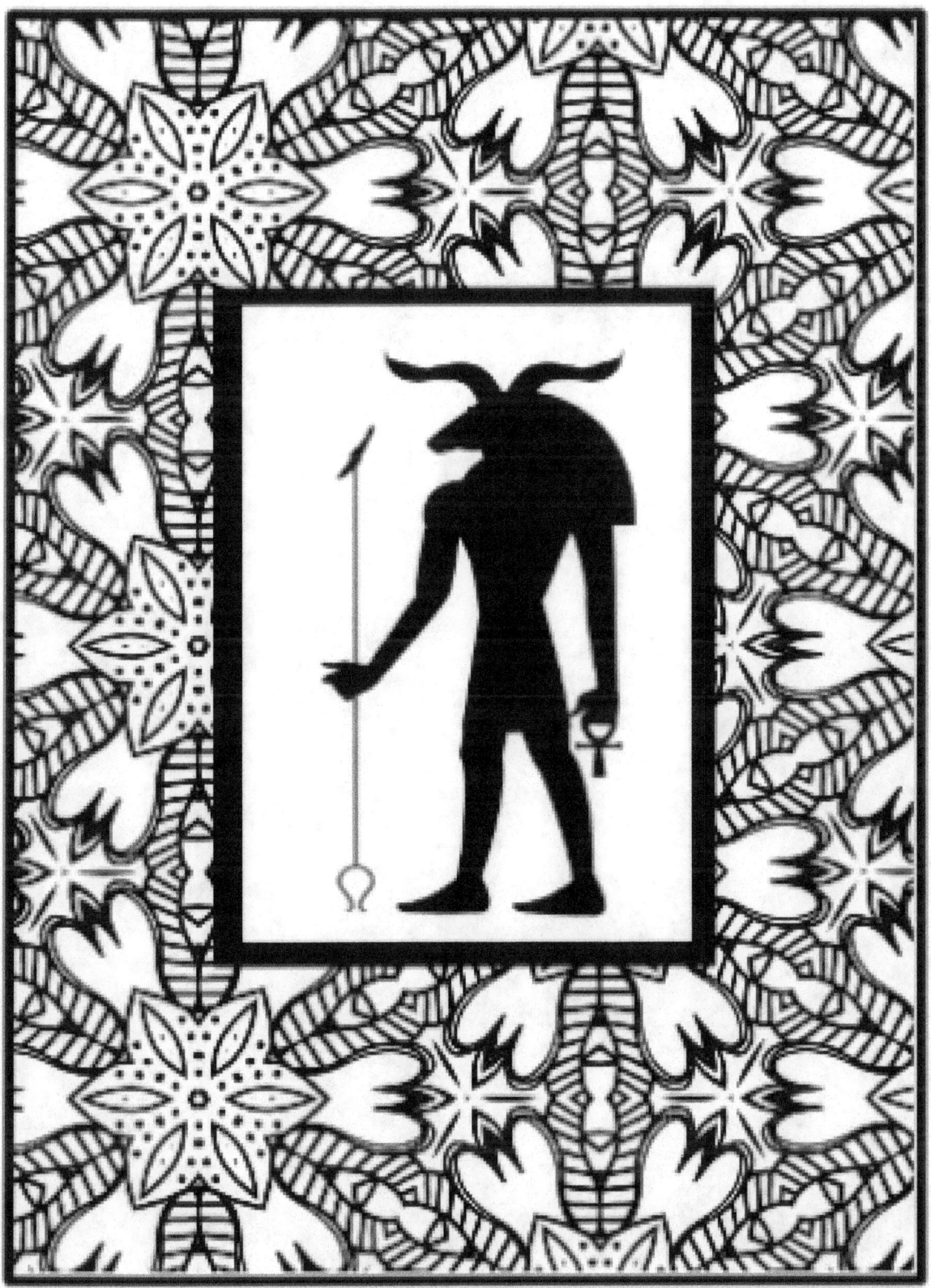

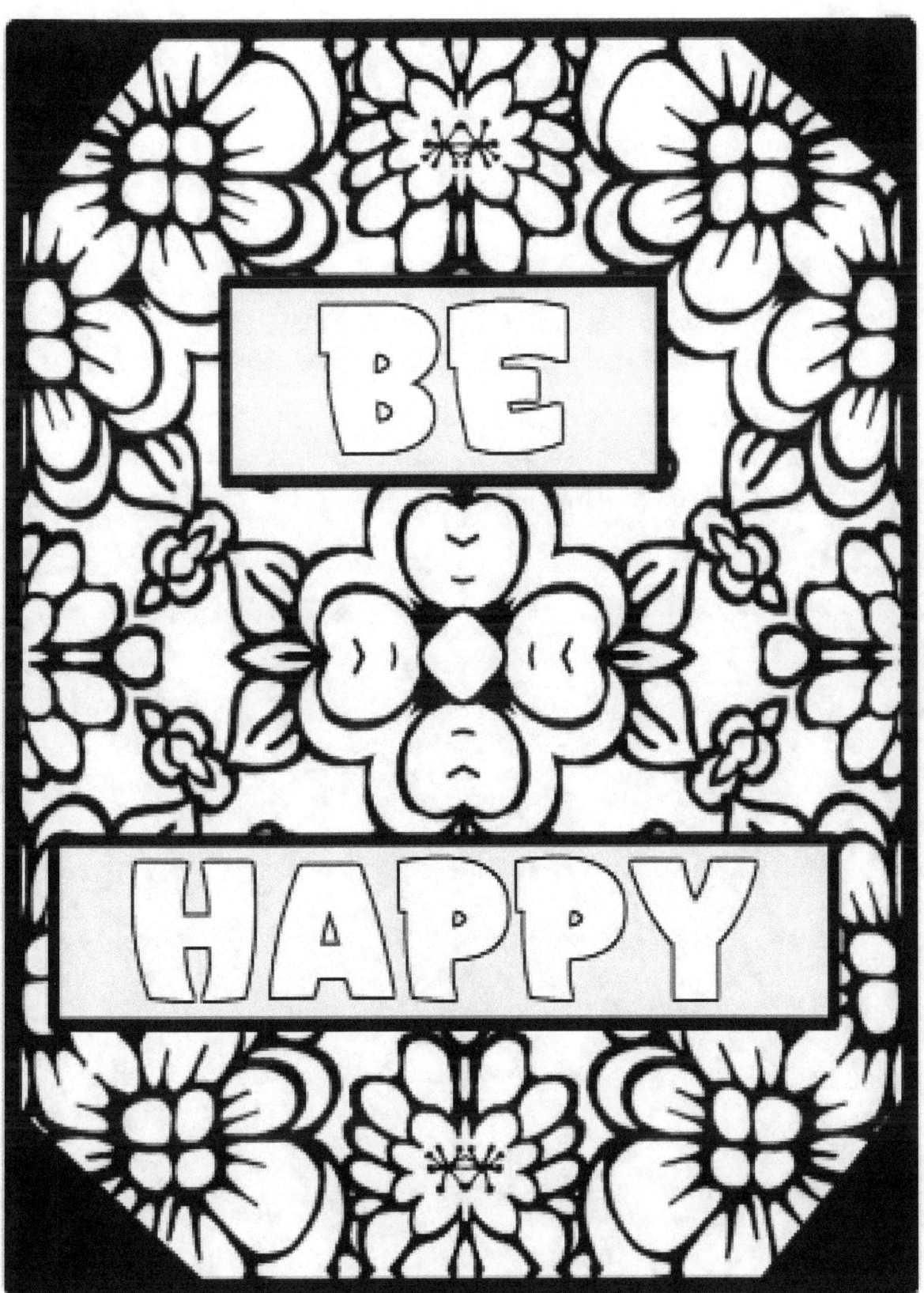

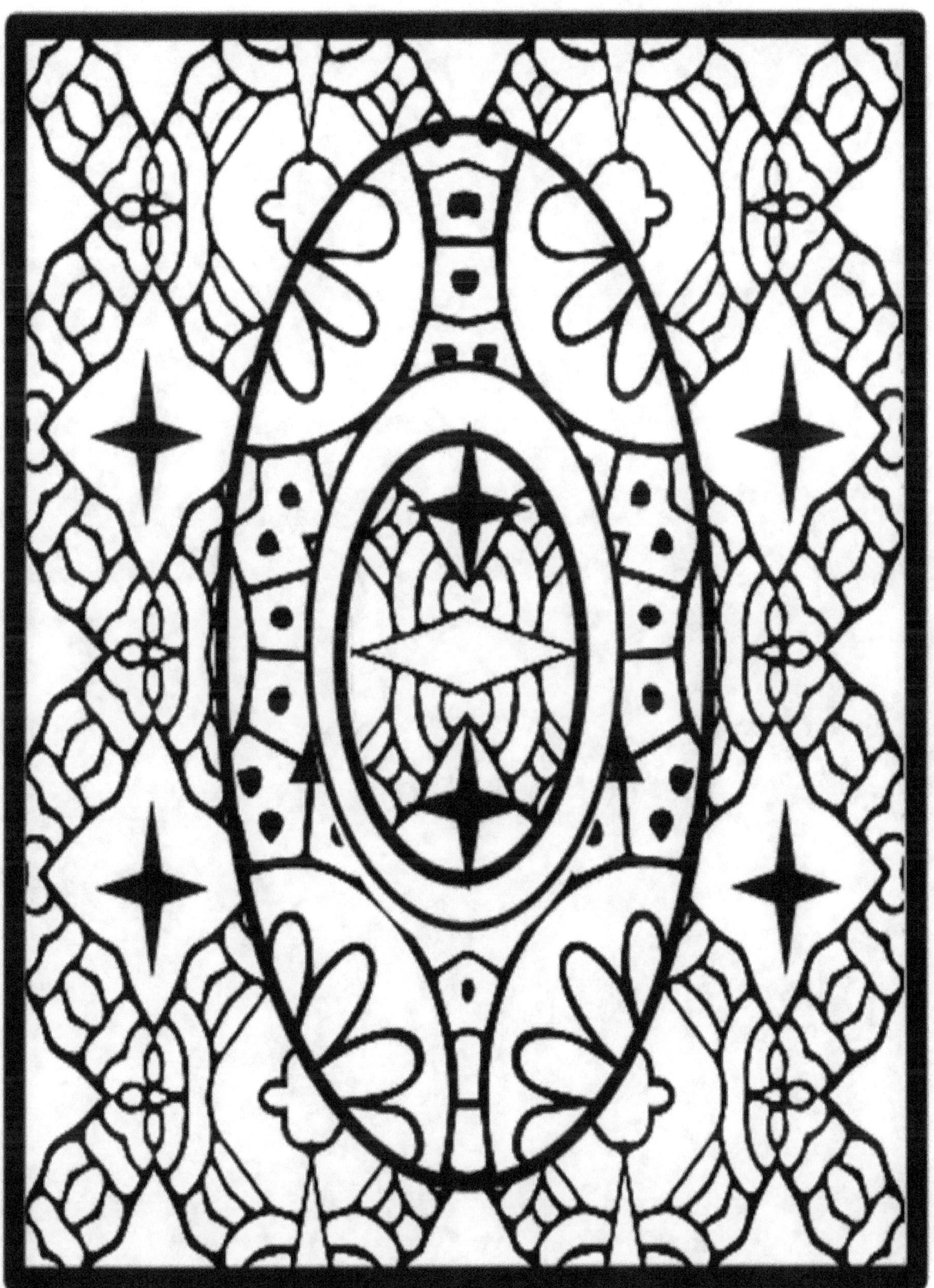

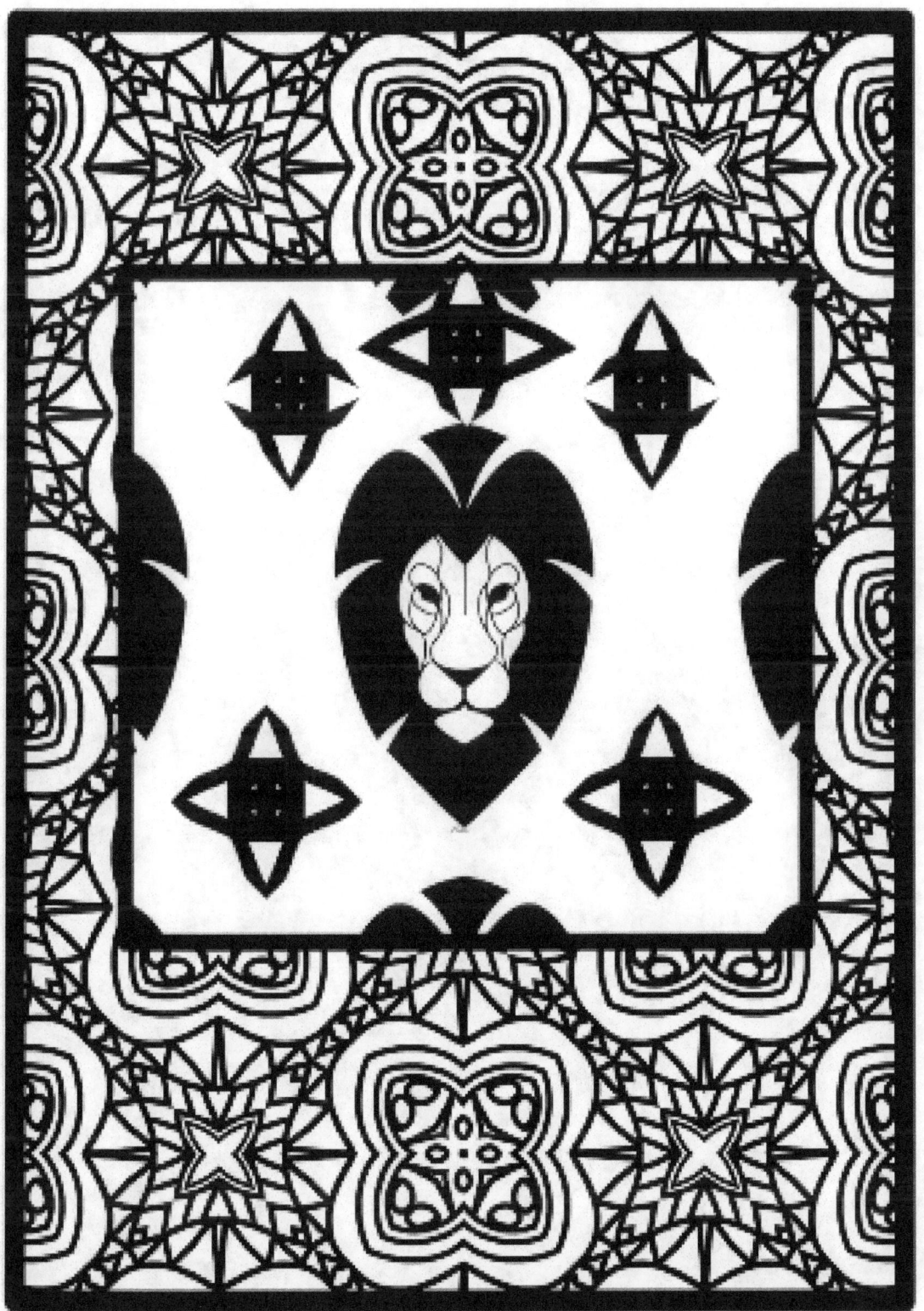

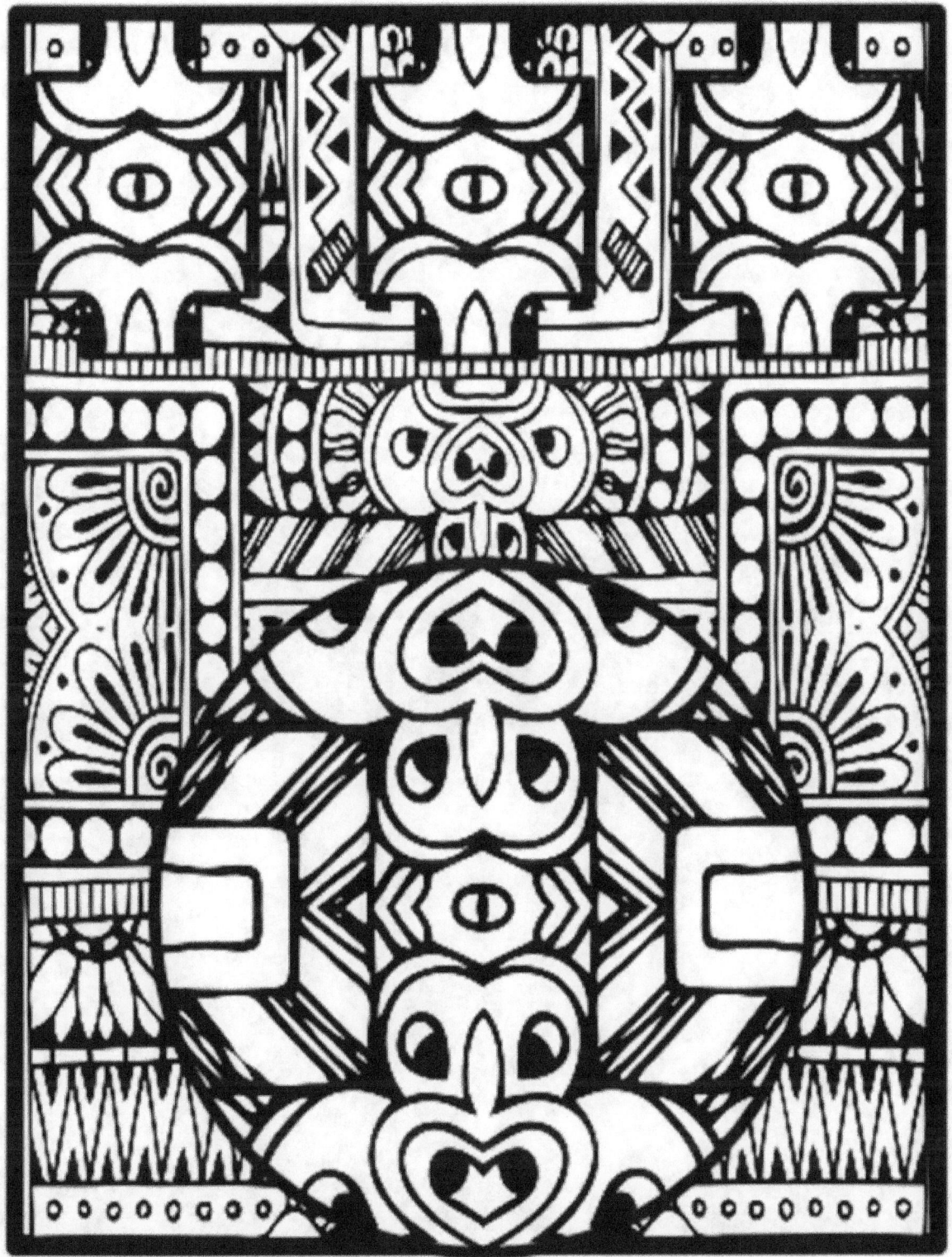

www.ingramcontent.com/pod-product-compliance
Lightning Source LLC
Chambersburg PA
CBHW080824170526
45158CB00009B/2516

* 9 7 8 1 0 8 6 6 5 8 5 3 8 *